Word 2002

Level 3

Susan L. Reber

Word 2002 : Level 3

Part Number: 084302
Course Edition: 3.2

ACKNOWLEDGMENTS

Project Team

Curriculum Developer and Technical Writer : Susan L. Reber • **Content Manager** : Cheryl Russo • **Technical Editor** : Elizabeth M. Swank • **Print Designer** : Daniel P. Smith

NOTICES

HELP US IMPROVE OUR COURSEWARE

Your comments are important to us. Please contact us at Element K Press LLC, 1-800-478-7788, 500 Canal View Boulevard, Rochester, NY 14623, Attention: Product Planning, or through our Web site at **http://support.elementkcourseware.com.**

This logo means that this courseware has been approved by the Microsoft® Office Specialist Program to be among the finest available for learning Microsoft Word 2002. It also means that upon completion of this courseware, you may be prepared to take an exam for Microsoft Office Specialist qualification.

What is a Microsoft Office Specialist? A Microsoft Office Specialist is an individual who has passed exams for certifying his or her skills in one or more of the Microsoft Office desktop applications such as Microsoft Word, Microsoft Excel, Microsoft PowerPoint, Microsoft Outlook, Microsoft Access, or Microsoft Project. The Microsoft Office Specialist Program typically offers certification exams at the "Core" and "Expert" skill levels. The Microsoft Office Specialist Program is the only program in the world approved by Microsoft for testing proficiency in Microsoft Office desktop applications and Microsoft Project. This testing program can be a valuable asset in any job search or career advancement.

To learn more about becoming a Microsoft Office Specialist, visit **www.microsoft.com/officespecialist**. To learn more about other Microsoft Office Specialist approved courseware from Element K, visit **www.elementkcourseware.com**.

*The availability of Microsoft Office Specialist certification exams varies by application, application version, and language. Visit **www.microsoft.com/officespecialist** for exam availability.

Microsoft, the Microsoft Office Logo, PowerPoint, and Outlook are trademarks or registered trademarks of Microsoft Corporation in the United States and/or other countries, and the Microsoft Office Specialist Logo is used under license from owner.

Element K is independent from Microsoft Corporation, and not affiliated with Microsoft in any manner. This publication may be used in assisting students to prepare for a Microsoft Office Specialist Exam. Neither Microsoft, its designated program administrator or courseware reviewer, nor Element K warrants that use of this publication will ensure passing the relevant exam.

NOTES

WORD 2002 : LEVEL 3

CONTENTS

LESSON 6: MODIFYING AN HTML PAGE

APPENDIX A: MICROSOFT OFFICE SPECIALIST PROGRAM

NOTES

ABOUT THIS COURSE

You know how to use Microsoft Word to create and format documents and newsletters. In this course, you'll learn how to use Word to create forms and long documents as well as how to make it easier to display and work with those forms and long documents by using macros and colloborating.

At this point, you've likely mastered the basics in Word and can already use Word to create almost any document you want. But if you've ever wanted to go beyond the basics and become the resident Word expert at your workplace, then this course can help you achieve that.

Course Description

Target Student

This course is designed for someone who has extensive computer and Internet experience and wants to learn the more advanced features of Word 2002. It is also intended for those preparing to pursue certification as Microsoft Office User Specialists (MOUS) in Word.

Course Prerequisites

To ensure your success, we recommend you first take the following Element K course or have equivalent knowledge:

- *Word 2002: Level 1*
- *Word 2002: Level 2*

How to Use This Book

As a Learning Guide

Each lesson covers one broad topic or set of related topics. Lessons are arranged in order of increasing proficiency with *Microsoft Word*; skills you acquire in one lesson are used and developed in subsequent lessons. For this reason, you should work through the lessons in sequence.

We organized each lesson into results-oriented topics. Topics include all the relevant and supporting information you need to master *Microsoft Word*, and activities allow you to apply this information to practical hands-on examples.

You get to try out each new skill on a specially prepared sample file. This saves you typing time and allows you to concentrate on the skill at hand. Through the use of sample files, hands-on activities, illustrations that give you feedback at crucial steps, and supporting background information, this book provides you with the foundation and structure to learn *Microsoft Word* quickly and easily.

As a Review Tool

Any method of instruction is only as effective as the time and effort you are willing to invest in it. In addition, some of the information that you learn in class may not be important to you immediately, but it may become important later on. For this reason, we encourage you to spend some time reviewing the topics and activities after the course. For additional challenge when reviewing activities, try the "What You Do" column before looking at the "How You Do It" column.

As a Reference

The organization and layout of the book make it easy to use as a learning tool and as an after-class reference. You can use this book as a first source for definitions of terms, background information on given topics, and summaries of procedures.

Course Objectives

In this course, you will create, modify, and distribute forms, long documents, and Web pages.

You will:

- create and distribute a form.
- automate tasks by writing and revising macros.
- create references to information in a document.
- prepare a document for publication.
- revise documents based on feedback provided by other users.
- modify an HTML page in Word.

Course Requirements

Hardware

- Pentium 133 MHz or higher processor required for all operating systems.
- 64 MB of RAM recommended minimum for Windows 2000 Professional; in addition, you should have 8 MB of RAM for each application running simultaneously. (Note: Memory requirements may differ for other operating systems.)
- 600 MB of free hard-disk space. (Under Windows 2000, at least 4 MB of space must be available in the Registry.)
- Either a local CD-ROM drive or access to a networked CD-ROM driver for installation purposes.
- A two-button mouse, an IntelliMouse, or compatible pointing device.
- VGA or higher resolution monitor; Super VGA recommended.
- A sound card.
- A 9600 baud modem or higher. An Internet connection with access to the World Wide Web. The connection is necessary to complete some tasks and Web Tips throughout the book.
- A Microsoft Exchange Server if you plan to key optional Activity 5–3 "Distributing the Document for Review."

Software

- Microsoft Office XP Professional—see the Class Setup Requirements for setup instructions.
- An installed printer driver. (Printers are not required; however, each PC must have an installed printer driver to use Print Preview.)
- Microsoft Exchange, Internet SMTP/POP3, IMAP4, or other MAPI-compliant messaging software required for email features if you plan to complete optional Activity 5–3"Distributing the Document for Review."

Class Setup

 This course was written usign the Windows 2000 Professional operating system. Using this course with other operating systems may affect how the activities work.

The manufacturer states that Microsoft Office XP Professional with FrontPage will work with Microsoft Windows 98, Microsoft Windows ME, and Microsoft Windows NT Workstation 4.0. Office XP Professional with FrontPage will not run on the Microsoft Windows 3.x, Microsoft Windows NT 3.5x, or Microsoft Windows 95 operating systems.

1. Install Windows 2000 Professional on a newly formatted hard drive.
2. If the Getting Started With Windows 2000 window is open, uncheck the Show This Screen At Startup and click Exit.
3. Install a printer driver.

📌 A printer isn't necessary for class, but you must have a printer driver installed.

4. Perform a custom installation of Microsoft Office XP Professional with FrontPage.

   • On the Select The Office XP Applications You Would Like Installed page of the Setup Wizard, check Microsoft Word and Microsoft Outlook. (You can install all programs, if you prefer.)

   • Select the Choose Detailed Installation Options For Each Application check box and click Next.

   • From the Digital Signature For VBA Projects option under Office Shared Features, choose Run From My Computer.

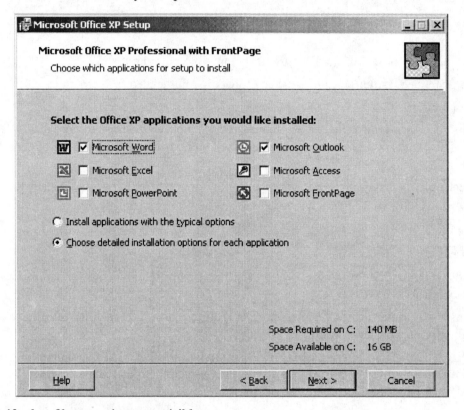

5. Verify that file extensions are visible.

   a. In Windows Explorer, choose View→Folder Options and select the View tab.

   b. If necessary, uncheck the Hide File Extensions For Known File Types option.

   c. Click OK and close Windows Explorer.

6. Verify that the Internet connection works. If a connection doesn't exist, from the Control Panel, double-click on Internet Options. In the Internet Properties dialog box, select the Connections tab. Click Setup to run the Internet Connection Wizard and select the proper settings.

7. In Word, minimize the Language bar, if necessary.

8. In Word, set the security level for macros to Medium.

   a. Choose Tools→Macro→Security.

   b. On the Security Level tab, select the Medium option.

   c. Click OK.

Class Setup for Activity 5-3 "Distributing a Document"

If you plan to key optional Activity 5-3, "Distributing the Document for Review," you will need to perform the following setup steps.

1. On the Exchange server, set up a user for each student.

    a. Delete all user names.

    b. Create a user name for the instructor (student00).

    c. Create a user name for each student (student01, student02, and so on).

2. Configure Outlook 2002.

    a. Double-click on the Microsoft Outlook shortcut on the Windows desktop.

    b. In the Outlook 2002 Startup dialog box, click Next.

    c. In the Account Configuration dialog box, E-mail Accounts, select Yes to configure an e-mail account, and click Next.

    d. In the Exchange Server Settings, Microsoft Exchange Server text box, type the name of the server you are using.

    e. In the User Name text box, type the user name.

    f. Click Next.

    g. Click Finish to close the Wizard.

3. In the Enter Password dialog box, type the user name, password, and domain name and click OK.

4. If an alert is displayed stating that the Microsoft Exchange Server is unavailable, click Retry.

5. On each student computer, log on to Windows using the student user name. You might need to create a profile for each user.

Before Every Class

1. Run the self-extracting data file located on the data disk. If necessary, set the path for the data files so that they extract to the My Documents folder for the user's profile (C:\Documents And Settings\USER Profile Name\My Documents.)

2. Move the template files (Property Inquiry.dot, Add Fields.dot, and Final Form Fields.dot) from the My Documents folder to the default User Templates directory for Word. (In Word, you can choose Tools→Options and display the File Locations tab to find out where the default Templates directory is.)

3. In Word, choose Tools→Customize and perform the following steps in the Customize dialog box.

    a. On the Options tab, click the Reset My Usage Data button.

    b. On the Toolbars tab, click the Reset button.

    c. If necessary, drag the Macros menu off the menu bar.

    d. Close the Customize dialog box.

NOTES

LESSON 1
Creating and Distributing Forms

Lesson Objectives:

In this lesson, you will create and distribute a form.

You will:

- Create a form template.
- Add fields to a form template.
- Protect a form so that users can enter information only in the fields on the form.
- Test and revise the finished form.

Introduction

You may find that during the course of your work day, you need to capture information from customers or co-workers. In this lesson, you will create forms that you can print or distribute.

Imagine that you work as a sales representative for a large company. You want to make your life a little easier, by ensuring that you have all the information you need by the time you get off the phone with a current or potential client. You could just ask a series of questions and write down the answers, or, you could create a form that you or your clients can fill out.

TOPIC A

Create a Form Template

The first step in creating a form is to create the template that is the basis for the form. In this topic, you'll create a form template.

If there is a lot of information you gather from many clients on a regular basis, form templates will make your life easier. They provide consistent formatting and ensure that you have all of the information you need in one place.

About Forms

Definition:

A *form* is a document used to collect information. Forms are used to capture and compile or file away, for further reference, information about a variety of subjects from many different people. Whether forms are paper-based or electronic, they contain boilerplate text—for example, the form title and labels—and *fields* (containers for variable information in the document).

Example:

In Figure 1-1, you can see an example of a Word form used to collect customer information. Notice that there are different types of fields depending upon the type of information you want to capture.

˙Property·Inquiry·Form¶

9/17/2001·2:47·PM¶

˙Client·Information↵

¶

Name:¤	Client's·name¤	¤
Address:¤	Street·address¤	¤
Phone:¤	¤	¤
Appointment:¤	10/1/2001·9:00·AM¤	¤
Buyer/Seller:¤	☐ → Buyer¶ ☐ → Seller↵ ¤	¤
Property·Type:¤	Single·Family¤	¤
Price·Range:¤	☐ → Less·than·100K¶ ◼ → 100K·-·150K¶ ☐ → 150K·-·200·K¶ ☐ → Over·200K¤	¤
↵	↵	¤
Amenities:¤	☐ → A/C¶ ☐ → Fireplace¶ ☐ → Pool¶ ☐ → Hot·Tub↵ ¤	
Comments:¤	Additional·Information¤	¤

Figure 1-1: *An example of a completed Microsoft Word form.*

Create a Form Template

Procedure Reference: Create Form Templates

An electronic form is really a template. After you create your form template, you open a new document based on the form template and then you fill in the form. To create a form template:

1. Plan your form. You need to decide what information you want to capture on your form and determine where you want that information to appear. You might want to design the form on paper before you create it in Word.

2. Create or open the document that is the basis for the form.

3. Add and format the form's boilerplate text. This includes the form title and labels for the information you want to capture.

4. Insert fields, as necessary, to capture the information you need.

5. Protect the form.

6. Save the form as a template.

7. Test the form.

OPTIONAL ACTIVITY 1-1

Creating the Form Template

Setup:

Microsoft Word is running and the data files have been installed in the My Documents folder.

Scenario:

As a real estate agent for Burke Properties, you take many phone calls from potential buyers and sellers. Currently, you write this information down in a notebook, which you carry with you everywhere. This works, but sometimes you don't get all the information you need and you're afraid that if you accidentally misplace your notebook, you'll lose all that information. Therefore, you've decided to create your own form. You know that you can use Word to create a template that you can use to create a new document when someone calls and asks for information. You have determined that your form needs the following information:

- a document title ("Property Inquiry");
- the date the document was created;
- the client's name, address, and phone number;
- whether they want to buy or sell;
- the type of property;
- the price range of the property; and
- the amenities.

In addition, you want a place in your form for additional comments. You've decided to call the template My Property Inquiry. You'll start in this activity by creating the Form heading, "Property Inquiry Form," and creating the static text for your form. When you're finished, your form should look like the one shown in Figure 1-2.

Property Inquiry Form

Client Information

Name:	
Address:	
Phone:	
Appointment:	
Buyer/Seller:	
Property Type:	
Price Range:	
Amenities:	
Comments:	

Figure 1-2: *The form template after adding static text.*

What You Do	How You Do It
1. In a new, blank document, **create the document title** *Property Inquiry Form*. (Use Heading 1 style to format the title.)	a. **Click the New Blank Document button.** b. **Type** *Property Inquiry Form*. c. Using the Styles And Formatting task pane or the Style drop-down list on the Formatting toolbar, **apply the Heading 1 style.**
2. Using Figure 1-2 as a reference, **create a Heading 2 style heading for** *Client Information*.	a. **Press [Enter] twice** to create a blank line. b. **Type** *Client Information*. c. Using the Style drop-down list on the Formatting toolbar, **apply the Heading 2 style.**

3. Using Figure 1-2 as a guide, on a new line below the Client Information heading, **create the table.**

   a. **Press [Enter]** to create a new blank line.

   b. **Choose Table→Insert→Table.**

   c. **Insert a table with two columns and nine rows.**

   d. **Set the width of the first column to 1.5 inches.**

   e. **Remove the borders from the table.**

   f. **Enter the following text in each cell in the first column:**

      Name:

      Address:

      Phone:

      Appointment:

      Buyer/Seller:

      Property Type:

      Price Range:

      Amenities:

      Comments:

   g. **Apply bold formatting to the first column.**

4. **Save the form as the *My Property Inquiry* template.**

   a. From the Save As Type drop-down list in the Save As dialog box, **select Document Template (*.dot)** to save the file as a template.

   b. **Name the new template *My Property Inquiry*.**

   c. **Verify that the file will be saved in the Templates folder.**

   d. **Click Save.**

TOPIC B

Insert Fields in a Form Template

After you design and lay out your form, you're ready to add fields for the information you want to capture. In this topic, you'll add several different types of fields to the form template.

A form without any place to enter information is not going to help you much in the long run. Before you can use the form, you need to add fields to it.

Form Fields

Definition:

Each Word form can hold a variety of form fields—fields that contain any information that might change from form to form. Form fields can contain data that users enter or actions that Word performs automatically. Form fields contain *field codes* used to tell Word what kind of information is contained in a field or what to do in that field.

Types of Fields

Table 1-1 describes some of the types of fields you can use in your forms.

Table 1-1: *Field Types for Forms*

Field Type	Description
Date And Time	A field that displays, in the format you choose, the date and/or the time that the document was created.
Fill-in	A field that displays a dialog box prompting respondents to enter information such as their name and address.
Text	A field on a form for typing in words, numbers, a date, the current date or time, or the results of a calculation.
Check Box	A field on a form that respondents can check to show that they agree or disagree with the choice. Use check boxes in surveys where you want to allow respondents to select more than one answer.
Drop-Down	A field on a form where respondents can choose one answer from a list of choices that drops down when they click on the down arrow to the right of the field.

Example:

Here is an example of each of the different types of fields.

Field Type	Example
Date And Time	DATE \@ "M/d/yyyy"

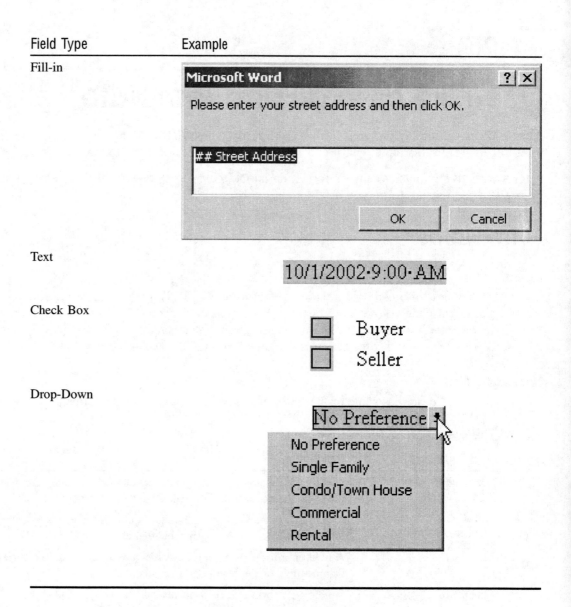

Field Type	Example
Fill-in	
Text	
Check Box	
Drop-Down	

Display Field Codes

When you enter a field in a document, Word displays either the field value or the field codes. Field codes are displayed in a document between curly braces—for example, {FORMTEXT}.

Generally, field codes take up a lot more space onscreen and are harder to decipher. Fortunately, you do not have to look at Word's field codes unless you want to. You can just choose to view the field's default value. To toggle field codes on and off, press [Alt][F9].

Add Fields to a Form Template

Procedure Reference: Add Fields to Form Templates

To add fields to a form template:

1. Place the insertion point in the location where you want to insert the field.

2. To use the Field dialog box to insert fields:

a.   Choose Insert→Field.

b.   From the Categories list box, select a category for the field you want to enter.

c.   From the Field Names list box, select the field you want.

d.   In the Field Properties section, set any field properties.

e.   In the Field Options section, set the desired options.

f.   Click OK.

3.   To use the Forms toolbar to insert fields:

a.   If necessary, display the Forms toolbar.

b.   Click the Form Field button you want.

c.   If necessary, click the Form Field Options button and set any options.

Date And Time Fields

To insert a Date And Time field:

1.   With the insertion point in the location where you want to insert the field, choose Insert→Field.

2.   If necessary, from the Categories drop-down list, select Date And Time.

3.   Select the type of Date And Time field you want to enter.

4.   In the Field Properties section, select a format from the Date Formats list box.

5.   Click OK.

Fill-in Fields

To insert a Fill-in field:

1.   With the insertion point in the location where you want to insert the field, choose Insert→Field.

2.   If necessary, from the Categories drop-down list, select All.

3.   From the Field Names list box, select Fill-in.

4.   In the Field Properties section, enter the prompt you want to appear in the dialog box.

5.   In the Field Options section, enter the default text you want Word to display in the dialog box.

a.   Check the Default Response To Prompt check box.

b.   In the text box, enter the text you want Word to display in the dialog box as the default.

6.   Click OK.

ACTIVITY 1-2

Inserting a Date And Time Field and Fill-In Fields in the Form Template

Data Files:

* Property Inquiry Template.dot

Setup:

If you did not complete the last activity, you can use Property Inquiry Template.dot to complete this activity.

Scenario:

You've created the layout for your form, and now you need to begin adding the fields to it. You think it would be nice to add a field that will automatically display the date the document was created so that it will be easy to tell how old the form is. You also want to insert fields that will ask users to enter the client's name, address, and phone number when they create a new document. Because you don't want to lose any of your changes, you save the template when you're finished.

What You Do	How You Do It
1. On the line below the document title, **insert a field that displays the document creation date.**	a. **Place the insertion point on the line below the document title.**
	b. **Choose Insert→Field** to open the Field dialog box.
	c. From the Categories drop-down list, **select Date And Time.**
	d. If necessary, in the Field Names list box, **select CreateDate.**
	e. In the Date Formats list box, **select the format of your choice.** Word displays your selection in the Date Formats text box.
	f. **Click OK** to insert the CreateDate field in your document.

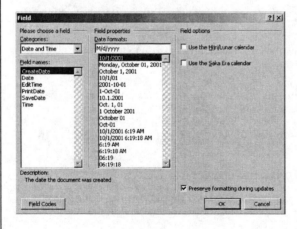

2. In the cell to the right of the Name label, **insert the fill-in field shown here.**

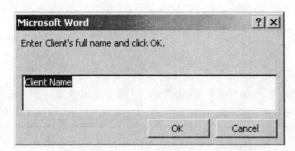

a. **Place the insertion point in the cell to the right of the Name label.**

Client Informati

| Name: | |

b. **Choose Insert→Field.**

c. From the Categories drop-down list, **select All** to display all the fields.

d. In the Field Names list box, **select Fill-in.**

e. In the Prompt text box, **type** *Enter Client's full name and click OK.*

f. In the Field Options section, **check the Default Response To Prompt check box** and type *Client Name*.

g. **Click OK twice** to close the Prompt dialog box and the Fields dialog box and return to the document.

3. **How can you display the field code?**

Save the template.

 If you used Property Inquiry Form.dot to complete this activity, make sure you save the template as My Property Inquiry.dot and overwrite the existing file, if necessary.

PRACTICE ACTIVITY 1-3

Adding Additional Fill-in Fields

Scenario:

You've entered a fill-in field for the client's name, but you also need to enter a fill-in field for the client's address and one for the phone number. When you're finished, save the template.

1. In the cell to the right of the Address label, **insert a fill-in field that asks the user to enter the client's address and then click OK.** The field should contain the default prompt "Street Address."

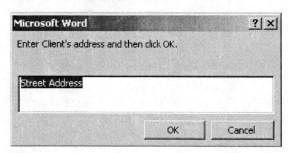

2. In the cell to the right of the Phone label, **insert a fill-in field that asks the user to enter the client's phone number and then click OK.** Don't include a default prompt.

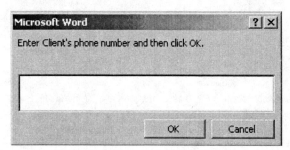

3. **Save the template.**

Form Fields

In addition to using the Fields dialog box to insert generic fields in the form template, you can also use the Form Field buttons on the Forms toolbar to insert form fields in your documents. Table 1-2 describes and displays the Form Field buttons on the Forms toolbar.

Table 1-2: *The Form Field Buttons on the Forms Toolbar*

Button	ScreenTip	What It Does
abl	Text Form Field	Inserts a text field.

Button	ScreenTip	What It Does
☑	Check Box Form Field	Inserts a check box field.
🗔	Drop-Down Form Field	Inserts a drop-down field.

Set Form Field Options

After you insert a form field, you can use the Form Field Options dialog box to set or change the properties for that field. To do so:

1. Select the form field for which you want to set properties.

2. Click the Form Field Options button 🗔 .

3. In the Form Field Options dialog box, set the options you want.

4. Click OK to close the dialog box.

ACTIVITY 1-4

Inserting Form Fields in the Form Template

Objective:

To add text fields, check box fields, and a drop-down field to the form template.

Data Files:

• Property Inquiry 2.dot

Setup:

Before starting this activity, you must move the template data files (*.dot) from the My Documents folder to the default location for Microsoft Word templates on your computer. See the course setup for instructions. Use Add Fields.dot for this activity.

Scenario:

You've added all the fields you need that are not available on the Forms toolbar. Now it's time to add form fields from the Forms toolbar. You've decided that the remaining fields should be the following types:

Field Label	Form Field Type
Appointment:	A text field containing a date and time in the format M/d/yyyy hh:mm am/pm with a default date.
Buyer/Seller:	A check box for Buyer and one for Seller.
Property Type:	A drop-down list containing the values: Single Family; Condo/Townhouse; Commercial; and Investment.
Comments:	A text form field containing regular text.

When you're finished, save the template as My Property Inquiry.dot and overwrite the existing file.

What You Do	How You Do It
1. In Add Fields.dot, in the cell to the right of the Appointment label, **insert a text form field that will display the date of the appointment with the format M/d/yyyy h:mm am/pm.** If you would like, include the date format as help text in the Status bar.	a. From the Templates folder, **open Add Fields.dot.**
	b. If necessary, **right-click on a toolbar and choose Forms**to display the Forms toolbar.
	c. In the cell to the right of the Appointment label, **click the Text Form Field button** `ab|` on the Forms toolbar.
	d. On the Forms toolbar, **click the Form Field Options button** to display the Text Form Field Options dialog box.
	e. From the Type drop-down list, **select Date.**
	f. From the Date Format drop-down list, **select M/d/yyyy h:mm am/pm.**
	g. **Click the Add Help Text button.**
	h. On the Status Bar tab, **select the Type Your Own option and type** *Enter the appointment date in the format M/d/yyyy h:mm am/pm.*
	● <u>T</u>ype your own: Enter the appointment date in the format M/d/yyyy h:mm am/pm
	i. **Click OK twice** to close the Form Field Text Help dialog box and the Text Form Field Options dialog box.

2. **Insert a text field for comments in which you can type an unlimited amount of text.**

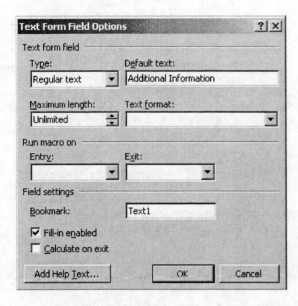

a. With the insertion point in the cell to the right of the Comments label, **click the Text Form Field button.**

b. **Double-click on the new field** to open the Text Form Field Options dialog box.

c. In the Default Text text box, **type *Additional Information.***

d. **Click OK.**

3. **For the Buyer/Seller information, enter the following Check Box form fields and labels.**

Buyer/Seller: ☐ Buyer
☐ Seller

a. With the insertion point in the cell to the right of the Buyer/Seller label, **click the Check Box Form Field button** .

b. **Press [Ctrl][Tab] to insert a tab.**

c. **Type *Buyer* and press [Enter].**

d. **Click the Check Box Form Field button, press [Ctrl][Tab], and then type *Seller*.**

4. In the cell to the right of the Property Type label, **add a Drop-Down Form Field** with the values: *Single Family, Condo/Townhouse, Commercial,* and *Investment.* When you're finished, **save the file.**

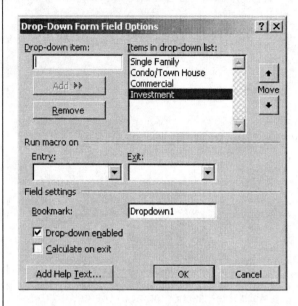

a. With the insertion point in the cell to the right of the Property Type label, **click the Drop-Down Form Field button** [icon].

b. **Click the Form Field Options button** [icon] **to open the Drop-Down Form Field Options dialog box.**

c. In the Drop-Down Item text box, **type *Single Family* and click Add** to add the text to the Items In Drop-Down List box.

d. **Type *Condo/Townhouse* and click Add.**

e. **Add *Commercial* and *Investment* to the Items In Drop-Down List box.**

f. **Click OK.**

g. **Save the file as *My Property Inquiry. dot*.** (Overwrite the existing file.)

PRACTICE ACTIVITY 1-5

Completing the Form Template

Scenario:

You've entered one of each type of form field. Now, you just need to finish the form by adding fields for Price Range and Amenities. Using Table 1-3 as a reference, complete the form template and save it.

Table 1-3: *Finishing the Form*

Field Label	Form Field Type
Price Range:	A check box for each of the following ranges: • Less than 100K • 100K - 150K • 150K - 200K • Over 200K

Field Label	Form Field Type
Amenities:	Check boxes for each of the following options:
	• A/C
	• Fireplace
	• Pool
	• Hot Tub

Your completed form template should look like the one shown in Figure 1-3.

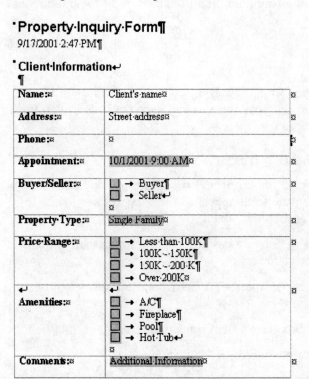

Property·Inquiry·Form¶
9/17/2001·2:47·PM¶

Client·Information↵
¶

Name:¤	Client's·name¤	¤
Address:¤	Street·address¤	¤
Phone:¤	¤	¤
Appointment:¤	10/1/2001·9:00·AM¤	¤
Buyer/Seller:¤	☐ → Buyer¶ ☐ → Seller↵ ¤	¤
Property·Type:¤	Single·Family¤	¤
Price·Range:¤	☐ → Less·than·100K¶ ☐ → 100K·-·150K¶ ☐ → 150K·-·200·K¶ ☐ → Over·200K¤	¤
↵	↵	¤
Amenities:¤	☐ → A/C¶ ☐ → Fireplace¶ ☐ → Pool¶ ☐ → Hot·Tub↵ ¤	
Comments:¤	Additional·Information¤	¤

Figure 1-3: *The completed form template.*

1. In the cell to the right of the Price Range label, **add a Check Box form field for each of the items listed in** Table 1-3.

2. In the cell to the right of the Amenities label, **add a Check Box form field for each of the items listed in** Table 1-3.

3. **Save the file.**

TOPIC C

Protect the Form

Once you've created your form template, you need to protect it to ensure that no one but you can make changes to it. In this topic, you will protect selected areas of your form.

You spent hours creating a form that contains all of the information you need. You sent the form, via email, to many of your clients so that you could update their information for your records. Unfortunately, you forgot to protect the form and didn't realize it until several clients sent it back and said the form was not easy to use.

Lock a Form

As you added fields to your form template, you might have noticed that you could not enter any information in the form fields. In order to see your form as end users will see it, you must first protect the form by locking the fields in place.

Procedure Reference: Lock a Form and Use a Password

To lock form fields in place, simply click the Protect Form button on the Forms toolbar. When you do so, the fields on the form appear as the user will see them. To unlock the fields, click the Protect Form button again.

For extra protection, you might want to assign a password to a form so that you can control when, and if, someone unprotects a form.

1. With the Form template open, choose Tools→Protect Document to open the Protect Document dialog box.

2. In the Protect Document dialog box, select the Forms option.

3. In the Password text box, enter a password for the document.

4. Click OK.

5. If necessary, confirm the password and click OK.

The Protect Document menu command is a toggle. Once you protect a document or form, you can unprotect it by choosing Tools→Unprotect Document.

ACTIVITY 1-6

Protecting the My Property Inquiry Form Template

Data Files:

- Final Form Fields.dot

Setup:

My Property Inquiry.dot is open. If you did not complete Practice Activity 1–5, use Final Form Fields.dot to complete this activity. At the end of the activity, save the file as My Property Inquiry.dot and overwrite the existing file.

Scenario:

You've completed the form, but you can't use it yet. There's one more step before you can begin using the form. You need to protect the form so that the only place users can enter information is in the fields. You notice the Protect Form button on the Forms toolbar and begin by using that to protect the form. It does lock the form, but when you send the form out to co-workers to review, you find out that they can easily unlock it by clicking the Protect Forms button again. You want to make sure that you're the only one who can unlock the form and make changes to it. Therefore, you decide to add a password to the form. When you're finished, save the template.

What You Do	How You Do It
1. What are some reasons you might want to protect a form?	
2. Protect the form so that you can only enter information in the fields.	a. If necessary, **display the Forms toolbar.**
	b. **Click the Protect Form button** .
3. How can you tell whether the form is protected or not?	

4. **Add a password to the form.**

   a. **Click the Protect Form button** 🔒 to unprotect the form.

   b. **Choose Tools→Protect Document** to open the Protect Document dialog box.

   c. In the Password text box, **enter a password for the form and click OK.**

   d. **Type the password again and click OK.**

5. **Now that you've entered a password for the form, what happens when you click the Protect Form button?**

   If necessary, **password protect the template again.**

   Save the template as *My Property Inquiry.dot.* (Overwrite the existing file, if prompted.)

Topic D

Test a Form

A form template isn't of very much use if it doesn't work the way you expect it to. Before you distribute your form to anyone or try to use it yourself, it's good practice to test it. In this topic, you'll test your form template.

You've just spent hours creating a form that will make it easier for you to do your job. Just as you're putting the finishing touches on the form, you get a call from an important client and decide to use your form before you've tested it. As you talk to the client, you begin filling in information on the form. You find that you're missing several fields and, because the form is protected, you can't add them to the document on the fly. So, you're stuck trying to sound like you're paying attention as you scramble for a piece of paper and pencil so you can write down the additional information you need. No one wants to lose information, so take the time to test your document before you release it to the general public.

Test and Revise the Form

Procedure Reference: Test Forms

To test your form:

1. With the form template still open, display the New Document task pane.

2. In the New From Template section, use the General Templates link and open a new document based on the form template.

3. Enter information in each field in the form.

4. Check each field to make sure that it includes all of the information you want to capture and that it looks the way you want it to look.

5. Document any changes you want to make to the form template.

6. Close the new document without saving.

Procedure Reference: Revise Forms

Based on the outcome of your test, you may want to make changes to your form. To revise your form:

1. In the form template, click the Protect Form button on the Forms toolbar to unlock the form.

    If necessary, enter the password and click OK.

2. Make the changes you documented during your test.

3. Protect the form again. (Either use the Tools→Protect Document command and set a password or click the Protect Form button.)

4. Save the template.

Distribute Forms

Once you've tested and revised your form, you're ready to distribute it. You might choose to print it and have users fill out the paper form. Or, you might place the form on a shared location, such as a network, and have users fill out the form electronically.

ACTIVITY 1-7

Testing and Revising the Form

Setup:

My Property Inquiry.dot is open.

Scenario:

You've just received a call from a potential client who has inherited some money and she wants to purchase some real estate. You decide this is a good opportunity to test and revise your form. During the course of your phone call, you find out the following information which you write down and then enter in your form:

- Her name is Lydia Rose.

- At this point, she doesn't have a preference for the type of property she would like to purchase. She's more concerned that the property be in her price range, which is less than $100,000.

- She would like to meet with you on the 22nd of this month at 9:00 am.

- She doesn't care what amenities the real estate has, as long as she likes the property.

- Her home address is 25 College Street.

- Her phone number is 716-555-1234.

Because there is some information you can't capture in your form as it is now, you need to make revisions to the form template. When you're finished making the changes you want, save and close the template. (You can close the test form without saving it.)

What You Do	How You Do It
1. In a new document based on the My Property Inquiry.dot template, **enter as much of the appropriate information from the scenario as you can into the form fields.**	a. **Choose File→New, and in the New Document task pane, click on the General Templates link.**
	b. On the General tab, **select My Property Inquiry.dot and click OK.**
	c. In the first Fill-in Field box, **type** *Lydia Rose* **and click OK.**
	d. In the second Fill-in Field dialog box, **type** *25 College Street* **and click OK.**
	e. In the third Fill-in Field dialog box, **type** *716-555-1234* **and click OK.**
	f. In the Appointment Date field, **enter the date and time of the appointment** (the 22nd of this month at 9:00 am).
	g. **Select the Buyer check box and the Less Than 100K check box.**

2. **Is there any information you couldn't enter?**

Close the test form without saving it.

3. In the form template, **edit the Drop-Down form field so that** *No Preferences* **appears at the top of the list of property types.**

a. On the Forms toolbar, **click the Protect Form button.**

   If necessary, **enter the password you set in the last activity, and click OK** to unlock the form.

b. **Double-click on the Drop-Down form field** to open the Options dialog box.

c. **Type** *No Preferences* **and click Add.**

d. In the Items In Drop-Down List box, **click the Move Up button until No Preferences appears at the top of the box.**

e. **Click OK.**

f. On the Forms toolbar, **click the Protect Form button** to lock the form.

g. **Save and close My Property Inquiry.dot.**

Lesson 1 Follow-up

Forms are useful for collecting information for a variety of reasons. In this lesson, you learned how to create and distribute forms.

1. **What are some ways you might use forms to make your job easier?**

2. **How will you distribute your forms?**

NOTES

LESSON 2
Automating Tasks

Lesson Objectives:

In this lesson, you will automate tasks by writing and revising macros.

You will:

- Run a pre-recorded macro.
- Record a macro.
- Edit an existing macro.
- Add a button to a toolbar.
- Create a custom menu.

Introduction

The more you use Word, the more likely it is that there are time consuming tasks that you do over and over again. In this lesson, you'll learn how to automate those tasks by writing and revising macros.

Suppose that you have to write a report for your manager each month. In that report, you have to quote and chart sales figures for the month. Those sales figures are stored in an Excel database. Each month, you have to open the Excel database, copy the sales figures, and paste them into your Word document, and then create a chart from those figures. It's time consuming and, furthermore, because you only do it once a month, by the time the monthly report rolls around, you usually spend a lot of time trying to figure out how to get all of the information you need. Wouldn't it be nice if you could just do it once and then have Word update the information for you each month? With a macro, you can.

TOPIC A

Run Macros

Before you begin creating your own macros, it's a good idea to familiarize yourself with macros by running one that has been created for you. In this topic, you'll run an existing macro.

At your company, you may be fortunate enough to have someone who creates macros for you. Those pre-recorded macros aren't very useful sitting on your network or hard drive. You need to know how to run them in order to make them useful.

Macros

Definition:

A *macro* is a stored series of instructions that you can run by invoking a single command. You can use macros to standardize complex and repetitive tasks. Macros can include keystrokes (function and shortcut keys) and mouse clicks (selections in dialog boxes, menus, and toolbars). However, mouse movements, such as using the mouse to select a word in the document window itself, cannot be recorded.

Example:

You can create a macro that does something as simple as format the text in a selected paragraph or as complex as writing and formatting a standard business letter. In the second case, the macro might enter standard text, insert the current date, and prompt you for the name and address of the person to whom you want to send the letter, and then type and format the rest of the letter.

Run a Macro

Procedure Reference: Run an Existing Macro

To run an existing macro:

1. Choose Tools→Macro→Macros to open the Macros dialog box.

2. If necessary, from the Macros In drop-down list, select the template where the macro is stored.

3. In the Macro list box, select the macro you want to run.

4. Click the Run button.

Security Level for Macros

When you open a document, Word determines whether the document contains any macros. If the document does not contain any macros, Word opens it without any warnings. If the document contains macros, Word opens it based on the current security settings. You can specify whether you want Word to treat documents that contain macros with a high, medium, or low security level.

- High—Word allows only signed and trusted macros to run. Unsigned macros are disabled before the file opens. This is the default security setting.

- Medium—You receive a prompt asking whether you want to enable or disable macros in the file when you open a file containing macros.

- Low—Word opens all files (even those containing macros) without any warning.

ACTIVITY 2-1

Running a Pre-recorded Macro

Data Files:

- Automate Tasks.doc

Setup:

Before starting this activity, you must set the security level for macros to Medium. See the course setup for instructions.

Scenario:

Burke Properties, Inc. recently changed and trademarked the company name. The company wants all literature and correspondence sent by every employee to consistently use the new name and trademark correctly. Your manager asked you to update all the company literature and correspondence you've created to reflect the new name and trademark. Because you have a lot of literature and correspondence, you were afraid this job would take forever. Fortunately, your technical support team created a macro called NameChange that does the work for you. All you have to do is open a document and run the macro. You only have one document left to fix. When you are finished, save the document as My Automate.

What You Do	How You Do It
1. If necessary, **enable macros in Automate Tasks.doc.**	a. **Open Automate Tasks.doc.**

LESSON 2

b. **Click the Enable Macros button.**

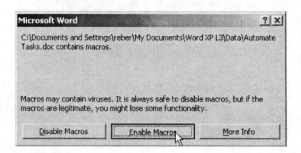

---

2. **How is the company referred to in the document?**

---

3. **Run the NameChange macro.**

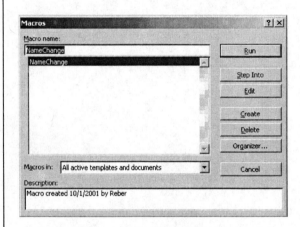

a. **Choose Tools→Macro→Macros** to open the Macros dialog box.

b. If necessary, **select NameChange.**

c. **Click the Run button** to execute the macro.

---

4. **Now how is the company referred to throughout the document?**

In the My Documents folder, **save the file as *My Automate*.**

TOPIC B

Record a Macro

It's nice to know how to run a macro that already exists, but unfortunately, most of us don't have someone sitting around creating macros for us. In this topic, you will record your own macro.

If you have a task that you perform over and over again—for example, adding a special header and footer to the documents you create—then recording a macro to do the work for you can save you time and also ensure that the task is done the same way each time.

Planning a Macro

You have a task that you do over and over (for example, sorting data in a table). It's time-consuming and you think it might be a good candidate for a macro. Before you record your macro, it's a good idea to spend some time figuring out exactly what you want the macro to do.

- Carefully plan the steps and commands you want the macro to perform. You might begin by writing down the steps you want the macro to perform in the order that you want the macro to execute them.

- Rehearse the macro.

  — Make sure that you know the keyboard shortcuts you need to use.

  — Walk through the steps at least once before you record the macro.

- Make sure your macro does not depend on the content in the current document. If it does, the macro will only be useful in that document.

If you take the time to plan and practice your macros, there will be fewer surprises when you record the macro, and it is less likely that you will have to edit or re-record the macro.

Record a Macro

Procedure Reference: Record a Macro

Once you have decided exactly what you want your macro to do and rehearsed the steps, you are ready to record the macro. To record a macro:

1. If necessary, open a document.

2. Open the Record Macro dialog box by:
   - Double-clicking on the grey REC indicator in the Status bar.
   - Choosing Tools→Macro→Record New Macro.
   - Displaying the Visual Basic toolbar and clicking the Record Macro button ⏺ .

3. In the Macro Name text box, enter a name for the macro.

   A macro name must begin with a letter and can only contain letters, numbers, and the underscore character (no spaces or special characters are allowed).

4. In the Assign Macro To section, assign the macro to a toolbar or keyboard shortcut.

5. From the Store Macro In drop-down list, select the location where you want to store the macro.

   By default, Word stores macros in the Normal template so that they are available in all documents. However, you can store the macro in the active document or in the template on which the active document is based.

6. In the Description text box, enter a description for the macro. This is the description you will see when you the select the macro in the Macros dialog box.

7. Click OK. Word displays the Stop Recording toolbar and attaches a mini-cassette tape below the mouse pointer.

8. Enter the commands and actions that your macro requires in the order in which you want Word to execute them for the macro.

   As you record the macro, you can:
   - Use the mouse to select menu commands, but not to select text.
   - Use the keyboard to select text.
   - Click the Pause button **||●** to stop recording for a little while (for example, to perform some keystrokes you don't want to record).
   - Click the Resume Recorder button **||●** to begin recording again.

9. Click the Stop Recording button on the toolbar **■** or double-click on REC on the Status bar when you have finished recording the macro.

10. Test the macro by running it in a new document.

ACTIVITY 2-2

Recording a Macro

Setup:
My Automate.doc is open.

Scenario:
Along with the new name, Burke Properties also has a custom footer the company wants you to use when you create documents for distribution to the public. Instead of creating the footer yourself each time you create a document, you decide to record a macro called BurkeFooter that will be available in all new documents and will do the work for you. When you're finished, your footer should look like the one shown in Figure 2-1.

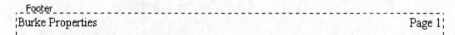

Figure 2-1: *The Burke Properties custom footer.*

What You Do	How You Do It
1. In the Record Macro dialog box, **name the macro and give it a description.**	a. On the Status bar, **double-click on the gray REC indicator** REC .
	b. In the Macro Name text box, **type** *BurkeFooter*.
	c. In the Description text box, **type** *Creates the standard Burke Properties footer*.
	d. **Click OK.**

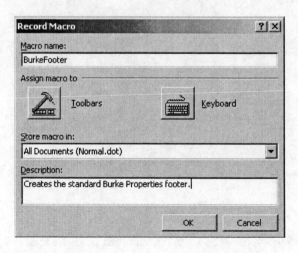

Lesson 2: Automating Tasks   31

2. Record the macro.	a. Choose View→Header And Footer.
	b. Click the Switch Between Header And Footer button ▣.
	c. Type *Burke Properties*.
	d. Press [Tab] twice.
	e. Type *Page* and press [Spacebar].
	f. Click the Insert Page Number button ▣.
	g. Click the Close button.
	h. Click the Stop Recording button ▪.
3. Test the macro.	a. Open a new, blank document.
	b. **Run the BurkeFooter macro** to verify that the footer looks like the one shown in Figure 2-1.
	c. Close the document without saving.

TOPIC C
Edit a Macro

Once you've created your macro, you might find that you need to make changes to it. Instead of recording the macro all over again, you can edit an existing macro. You'll learn how in this topic.

You want to create a macro that inserts a specially formatted table with three rows and three columns including a formatted header row containing text in your document at the location of the insertion point. You record the macro once and realize that you misspelled one of the words in the header row, so you record the entire macro again only to find that this time, you forgot a letter in a different word. If you just want to make minor changes to a macro (like adding a few words or correcting a misspelling), instead of recording the entire macro over and over, you can save time and spare yourself frustration by editing the macro.

The Visual Basic Editor

In Word, macros are created using Visual Basic for Applications (VBA). Therefore, editing a macro requires opening the Visual Basic Editor and editing code. While this isn't hard to do, it can be a little overwhelming at first. (See Table 2-1 and Figure 2-2.)

Table 2-1: *The Components of the Visual Basic Editor*

Component	Description
Project Explorer	On the left side of the Visual Basic Editor, the Project Explorer contains a list of all documents and template projects currently open. The Normal template is listed first as "Normal." Any other open documents or templates in use are listed in the Project Explorer as Project (Document_name) or TemplateProject (Template_name).
Project	Any open document or template other than the Normal template.
Modules	Where the macros are stored.
Code Window	On the right side of the Visual Basic Editor, the Code window displays the code for the macros stored in the module selected in the Project Explorer.

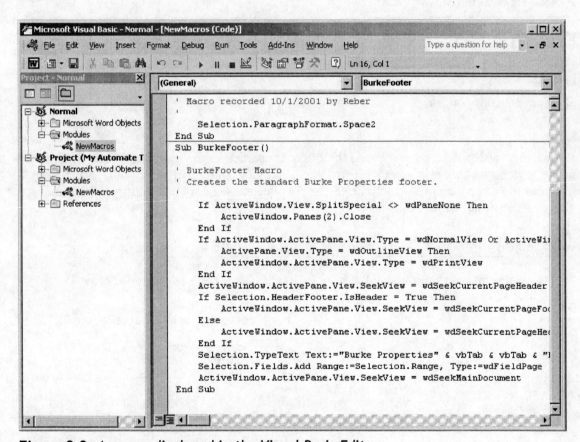

Figure 2-2: *A macro displayed in the Visual Basic Editor.*

Edit Macros

Procedure Reference: Edit an Existing Macro

As you test your macro, you note the things you need to change. If they are not significant, you might want to edit the macro instead of recording the entire macro again. To edit an existing macro:

1. Open a document based on the template in which the macro is stored.

2. Choose Tools→Macro→Macros.

3. Select the macro you want to edit and click the Edit button.

4. In the Code window in the Visual Basic Editor, make any changes in the Visual Basic for Applications code.

5. Choose File→Close And Return To Microsoft Word.

6. Test the macro by running it in a new document.

ACTIVITY 2-3

Editing a Macro

Setup:

My Automate.doc is open.

Scenario:

Just as you finish your macro to create the Burke Properties footer, management sends a new memo saying that they also want the text "We'll find the right property for you!" in the footer. You plan to record the entire macro again, but a colleague suggests that you try editing the macro in the Visual Basic Editor instead.

What You Do	How You Do It
1. **Open the macro in the Visual Basic Editor.**	a. **Choose Tools→Macro→Macros.**
	b. If necessary, **select BurkeFooter.**
	c. **Click the Edit button.**

2. **Using Figure 2-2 as a guide, identify the components of the Visual Basic Editor.**

___ Code window   ___ Project Explorer

___ Project   ___ Modules

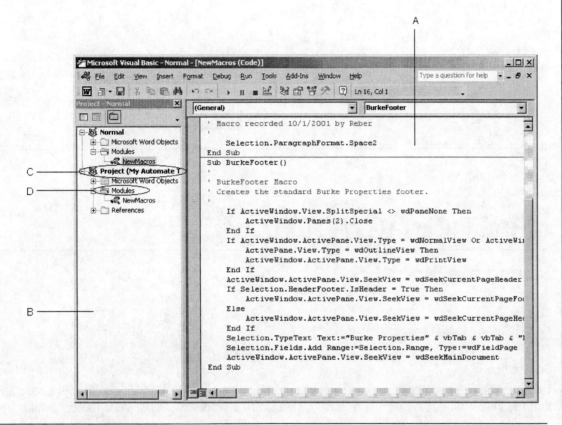

3. After Burke Properties, **add the text:** *We'll find the right property for you!*

     a. In the Code window, **find** `Selection.TypeText Text:="Burke Properties"`.

     b. **Place the insertion point after the *s* in 'Properties."**

         `Selection.TypeText Text:="Burke Properties"`

     c. **Type : and press [Spacebar].**

     d. **Type *We'll find the right property for you!***

4. **Remove one of the tab marks and close the Visual Basic Editor.**

a. **Select the first "& vbTab"** (immediately following the text you entered in the last step).

```
property for you!"  & vbTab  & vbTab
```

b. **Press [Delete].**

c. **Choose File→Close And Return To Microsoft Word.**

PRACTICE ACTIVITY 2-4

Testing the Macro

Setup:

My Automate.doc is open.

Scenario:

Because you've made changes to the macro, you decide that it is a good idea to make sure that the macro works the way you think it should. If it works correctly, your footer should look like the one shown here.

```
Footer
Burke Properties: We'll find the right property for you!                    Page 1
```

1. **Open a new blank document and run the BurkeFooter macro.**

2. **Check the footer to make sure the slogan has been added.**

3. **Close the file without saving.**

TOPIC D

Create Toolbar Buttons

You know that you can always access every command through Word's menus, but that isn't always convenient. If you use it enough, you might find that you want to add a command, AutoText entry, or macro to a toolbar. In this topic, you'll add a macro as a button to a toolbar.

If there is a menu command, macro, or AutoText entry that you access through Word's menus and that you use frequently, you'll quickly decide it's a good idea to streamline using that macro, command, or AutoText entry. You can eliminate extra keystrokes by adding Word objects as buttons to a toolbar.

Create a Toolbar Button

Although Word's toolbars adapt to show only the buttons you use most frequently, you might find that the command you want isn't attached to a toolbar button. Fortunately, you can create your own toolbar button by attaching a command, an AutoText entry, or a macro to a button, and adding that button to a toolbar.

Procedure Reference: Create a Button and Attach It to a Toolbar

To create a button and attach that button to a toolbar:

1. Choose Tools→Customize to open the Customize dialog box.

2. If necessary, display the Commands tab.

3. From the Categories list box, select a category to display the commands associated with that category.

4. From the Commands list box, select the command for which you want to create a button.

5. Drag the command from the Commands list up to the toolbar on which you want it to appear. As you move the mouse pointer over the toolbar, the I-beam shows you where Word will place the command when you release the mouse button.

6. In the Customize dialog box, click the Modify Selection button and make any changes to the button. You can:

   • Select the text in the Name text box and enter a new name for the button.

   • Use the Change Button Image palette to attach an image to the button.

   • Select a button style from the available options (Default Style—image only; Text Only; or Image And Text).

7. Click Close to close the Customize dialog box.

ACTIVITY 2-5

Assigning a Macro to a Toolbar Button

Setup:

My Automate.doc is open.

Scenario:

Because of a new company policy requiring that you include the Burke Properties footer in each company document you create, you recorded a macro, BurkeFooter, to create the footer for you.

When you recorded the macro, you didn't think it was important to add the macro to a toolbar because you didn't think you would use the macro that much. Since you recorded the macro, however, you've created several documents and find that it's a hassle opening the Macros dialog box each time you want to run the macro. You've decided to assign the macro to a button on the Standard toolbar so that you can run the macro by clicking on the toolbar button.

When you are finished, the Standard toolbar should look like the one shown in Figure 2-3.

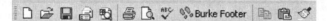

Figure 2-3: *The BurkeFooter macro button on the Standard toolbar.*

What You Do	How You Do It
1. **Assign the BurkeFooter macro to a new button on the Standard toolbar.**	a. **Choose Tools→Customize, and display the Commands tab.**

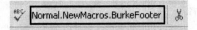

b. In the Categories list box, **select Macros** to display the available macros in the Commands list box.

c. In the Commands list box, **select Normal. NewMacros.BurkeFooter.**

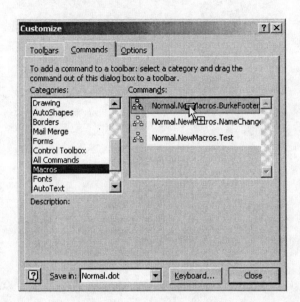

🖈 You should only see the BurkeFooter macro in the Commands dialog box.

d. **Drag the macro to the Standard toolbar after the Spelling And Grammar button.**

2. **Modify the button so that it looks like the one shown here.**

a. With the new toolbar button still selected, **click the Modify Selection button in the Customize dialog box** to display the menu.

b. **Select the text in the Name text box.**

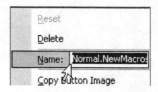

c. **Type** *Burke Footer*.

d. From the Modify Selection menu, if necessary, **choose Change Button Image and click on the footsteps.**

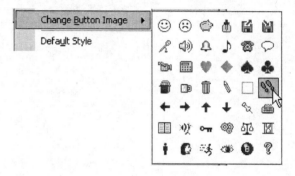

e. From the Modify Selection menu, **choose Image And Text** to display the button as an image and text.

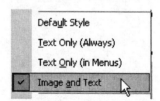

f. In the Customize dialog box, **click the Close button** to close the dialog box.

Remove Buttons from Toolbars

You can remove both custom buttons and default buttons from the toolbars. To remove a custom button, choose Tools→Customize and drag the button off the toolbar and down into the text area.

If you no longer want a default button on a toolbar:

1. On the toolbar that contains the button you want to remove, click the Toolbar Options button.

2. Choose Add Or Remove buttons.

3. From the submenu, choose the toolbar from which you want to remove the button.

4. Click the button you want to remove.

5. Click anywhere in the Word window to close the menus.

You can also remove custom buttons from toolbars. To do so, open the Customize dialog box and drag the toolbar button down off the toolbar.

OPTIONAL DISCOVERY ACTIVITY 2-6

Removing Buttons from the Standard Toolbar

Setup:
My Automate.doc is open.

Scenario:
Now that you've added a button to the Standard toolbar, you realize that there are many buttons on the Standard toolbar that you never use. You decide to remove a button or two that you never use.

1. **Remove the Hyperlink button from the Standard toolbar.**

2. **Remove the button of your choice from the Standard toolbar.**

TOPIC E

Create Custom Menus

You know how to add a button to a toolbar, but suppose you don't like using the toolbar and want to create your own menu. In this topic, you'll create a custom menu.

Chances are the commands you use most frequently are found in several different menus. It may be difficult to remember which menu holds which commands. If you would like, you can create your own menu and add all of the commands you use the most to that menu. Then, instead of searching in vain through several adaptable menus, you only have to look in one menu for the commands you want.

Create a Menu

Procedure Reference: Create a Custom Menu

If you prefer to use Word's menus, you can create custom menus that contain only the commands you select. To create a custom menu:

1. Choose Tools→Customize, and display the Commands tab.

2. From the Categories list box, select New Menu.

3. In the Commands list box, select New Menu and drag it to the menu bar. The I-beam indicates where the new menu will appear when you release the mouse button.

4. Rename the menu.

5. From the Commands tab of the Customize dialog box, add the commands you want to the menu.

6. Click OK to close the Customize dialog box.

You can delete a custom menu by opening the Customize dialog box and dragging the menu off the menu bar.

OPTIONAL DISCOVERY ACTIVITY 2-7

Creating a Custom Menu for Macros

Setup:

My Automate.doc is open.

Scenario:

You've decided that you like recording macros. They make life easier, and you know that you will continue to record macros. Running the macros from the Macros dialog box takes too much time, and if you add all the macros to the toolbar, you soon lose track of which button executes which macro. So, you decide to create a custom menu called Macros that will provide you with instant access to all of your macros. At this point, you have only the BurkeFooter macro.

1. **Before the Help menu, create a new menu called Macros.**

2. **Add the Burke Footer macro to the menu.**

3. **Use the menu to run the Burke Footer macro in a new blank document. When you're finished, close the document without saving changes.**

4. **Close My Automate.doc.**

Lesson 2 Follow-up

We all look for ways to make complex or menial tasks go quicker. One of Word's automation tools, the macro, can make it easier for you to complete many of the tasks that you perform on a regular basis. In this lesson, you learned how to write, revise, and execute macros. You also learned how to quickly access macros and other commands by adding them to toolbars and menus.

1. **What are some tasks that you perform on a regular basis that you might be able to automate by using a macro?**

2. **Are there some tasks you perform that it doesn't make sense to automate? Why or why not?**

NOTES

LESSON 3
Referencing Document Information

Lesson Objectives:

In this lesson, you will create references to information in a document.

You will:

*   Set a bookmark.
*   Insert footnotes and endnotes in a document.
*   Add captions to figures.
*   Create a cross-reference.

Introduction

At times, you might find it necessary to find and refer to information in your documents. In this lesson, you will learn various techniques for referring to information in your documents.

Imagine that you've spent a lot of time researching and writing the information in a long report. You want to make it easy for you and others to quickly find important information in the report. You also want to make sure that you give credit where credit is due. Creating document references ensures that your readers know what you're referring to and who your source is.

TOPIC A

Insert Bookmarks

The first step in creating references to information in a document is to find the text you want to reference. In this topic, you'll set bookmarks to mark specific locations in the document.

You're working your way through a long document, checking it for accuracy. You've been working for a long time and decide that it's time for a coffee break. You're going to close the document, because that's company policy; however, when you get back, you don't want to have to waste time scrolling through the entire document trying to find your place; so you set a bookmark. That way, when you get back to your desk, you can open the document and go right to the section you were working on when you left.

Bookmarks

A *bookmark* is a placeholder used to mark a location in a document so that you can quickly return to that location. You can bookmark multiple locations in a document, but each bookmark must have a unique name.

A Word bookmark is like a paper bookmark you use to mark your place in a book you're reading. When you put down the book, you insert the bookmark so you'll be able to find your page the next time you open the book.

Set Bookmarks

Procedure Reference: Set a Bookmark

To set a bookmark in a document:

1. Place the insertion point where you want to insert the bookmark (or select the text you want to bookmark).

2. Choose Insert→Bookmark to open the Bookmark dialog box.

3. In the Bookmark Name text box, enter a name for the bookmark. The bookmark name must be unique, begin with a letter, and cannot contain spaces.

4. Click the Add button.

If you no longer need a bookmark, you might want to delete it. You can delete a bookmark by selecting it in the Bookmark dialog box and clicking Delete.

Use Bookmarks

Once you insert a bookmark in a document, you can use it to quickly jump to the bookmark location. To use a bookmark, you can either use the Go To dialog box or the Bookmark dialog box to find the bookmark you want. To use the Go To dialog box to jump to a bookmark:

1. Choose Edit→Go To.

2. From the Go To What list, select Bookmark.

3. From the Enter Bookmark Name drop-down list, select the bookmark you want to jump to.

4. Click the Go To button.

To use the Bookmark dialog box to jump to a bookmark:

1. Choose Insert→Bookmark (or press [Ctrl][Shift][F5]).

2. Select the bookmark you want to jump to.

3. Click the Go To button.

View Bookmarks

It can be helpful to not only see where bookmarks are located in your document, but also to see what information, if any, is bookmarked. For instance, if you want to delete a paragraph, it would be nice to know if that paragraph contains a bookmark before you delete the paragraph text. To see the non-printing symbols that represent bookmarks in a document:

1. Choose Tools→Options.

2. On the View tab, in the Show options, select the Bookmarks option.

3. Click OK.

Brackets ([ ]) surround the bookmarked selection. If you don't make a selection before you insert a bookmark, then Word inserts empty brackets that look like an oversized capital letter I.

ACTIVITY 3-1

Creating a Bookmark

Data Files:

- Stockholder Report.doc

Scenario:

You're working on the Burke Properties Stockholder's annual report and your manager is getting ready to review it. Since she always wants to know the bottom line before she looks at anything else, you add a bookmark at the section that contains the review of the year's results. After you insert the bookmark, you decide to test it to make sure it's going to take your manager to the correct section of the document. Finally, as you were working on the document, you inserted your own bookmarks, one of which (growth) you want to remove before you send the document to your manager.

What You Do	How You Do It
1. In Stockholder Report.doc ,**bookmark the heading 'Review of Year Results."**	a. **Open Stockholder Report.doc.**
	b. At the top of page 4, **select the heading 'Review of Year Results."**
	c. **Choose Insert→Bookmark** to open the Bookmark dialog box.
	d. In the Bookmark Name text box, **type** *Year_Results* to name the bookmark.
	e. **Click the Add button.**

2. **Use the bookmark to move quickly to the 'Review of Year Results" heading.**

a. **Go to the beginning of the document.**

b. In the Find And Replace dialog box, **display the Go To tab.**

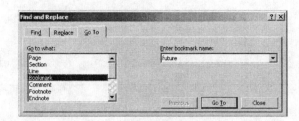

 Pressing [F5] is a shortcut for opening the Find And Replace dialog box and the Go To tab.

c. In the Go To What list box, **select Bookmark.**

d. From the Enter Bookmark Name drop-down list, **select Year_Results.**

e. **Click the Go To button** to jump to the Year_Results bookmark.

f. **Close the Find And Replace dialog box.**

3. **How many bookmarks are in the document?**

Can you tell by looking at the document that it contains bookmarks?

4. **Display the non-printing bookmark symbols for the Year_Results bookmark.**

a. If necessary, **go to the Year_Results bookmark.**

b. **Choose Tools→Options and select the View tab, if necessary.**

c. Under the Show section, **check Bookmarks.**

d. **Click OK.** Brackets surround the contents of the bookmark (in this case, the heading).

5. Delete the growth bookmark from the document.

    a. Choose Insert→Bookmark.

    b. From the Bookmark Name list, **select growth.**

    c. Click the Delete button.

    d. Close the Bookmark dialog box.

TOPIC B

Insert Footnotes and Endnotes

At some point, you might want to comment on or cite a reference for a particular piece of information in your document. In this topic, you will insert and modify footnotes and endnotes.

You are writing an article that you plan to have published in a trade magazine. As you are writing the article, you come across some published research that supports what you're talking about, so you add it to your article, but you forget to reference the source. Whether you intended to or not, you just took credit for someone else's work. You could find yourself in dire legal trouble if you refer to someone else's work without giving them credit.

Footnotes and Endnotes

Definition:

Footnotes and *endnotes* are notes that comment on or cite the reference for a particular fact in the text of a document. A superscript number in the document text indicates that there is a footnote or endnote for that text.

The only real difference between a footnote and an endnote is where they appear. A footnote appears at the bottom of the page containing the text it references, while an endnote appears at the end of the section or of the document containing the reference.

Example:

In Figure 3-1, you can see an example of a footnote and its corresponding reference in the document text.

REVIEW OF YEAR RESULTS

Financial

For the fiscal year ended June 30, total revenue increased 15% to $200.5 million from $174.3 million last year. Excluding non-recurring items[1], earnings before interest expense, income taxes, depreciation and amortization—a widely used measure of a company's ability to generate cash flow from operations—rose 127% to $15.3 million from $5.2 million a year ago.

Excluding a deferred tax benefit and other non-recurring expenses and extraordinary items, net income for the year was $10.6 million, an increase over the $1 million recorded last year. Fully diluted earnings per share on this basis increased to $.58 per fully diluted share, vs. $1.8 million, or a loss of $.08 per share, last year.

Non-recurring items in this fiscal year totaled $5.7 million. These include: a gain on the payoff of debt, net of taxes, of $4.6 million; other non-recurring expenses of $1.8 million

---

[1] Non-recurring items consist of deferred tax benefits.

Figure 3-1: *An example of a footnote in a document.*

Insert Footnotes and Endnotes

Procedure Reference: Insert a Footnote and an Endnote

You insert a footnote or an endnote whenever you want to provide additional supporting information or cite the source for a specific piece of information in your document.

1. Place the insertion point immediately after the text you want to comment on or reference.

2. Choose Insert→Reference→Footnote to open the Footnote And Endnote dialog box.

3. In the Location section, select either the Footnotes or the Endnotes option, and then from the drop-down list, select the location where you want the footnote or endnote to appear.

4. In the Format section, set the formatting options you want, if necessary.

5. Click Insert.

6. In the Footnote or Endnote area, type text for the footnote or endnote.

Guidelines

As you write documents, follow these guidelines to decide whether you need to add a footnote or an endnote.

- If you copy text from someone else's published work, you must use an endnote (or a footnote) to cite your source. If you don't, you are plagiarizing someone else's work.

- Use a footnote (rather than an endnote) to give a short explanation of some text in your document. Because a footnote appears on the same page as the text it refers to, readers are more likely to take the time to follow the link to the footnote.

- Use footnotes sparingly. Too many footnotes can distract readers.

ACTIVITY 3-2

Creating a Footnote

Setup:
Stockholder Report.doc is open.

Scenario:
After reviewing the Stockholder report, your manager asks you to add footnotes and endnotes to comment on some of the material in the report. In the Financial section, she wants you to add an explanation of non-recurring items at the bottom of the page. After the text "geographic reach, " she also wants you to add a reference to a note at the end of the document explaining that the geographic reach of Burke Properties covers eight states.

What You Do	How You Do It
1. In the first paragraph under the Financial heading, **insert a footnote for non-recurring items.**	a. **Find the text "non-recurring items."**
	b. **Place the insertion point immediately after the** *s* **in "items."**

---

[1] Non-recurring items consist of deferred tax benefits.

Financial

For the fiscal year ended
revenue increased 15% to
$174.3 million last year.
recurring items, earnings

	c. **Choose Insert→Reference→Footnote** to open the Footnote And Endnote dialog box.
	d. In the Location section, **verify that Footnotes is selected.**
	e. **Click Insert.**
	f. In the Footnote area, **type** *Non-recurring items consist of deferred tax benefits.*
2. In the document, **view the footnote reference in the text and note at the bottom of the page.**	a. **Double-click on the reference mark** to return to the document text.
	b. **Scroll down to the bottom of the page to view the footnote.** A line separates the footnote from the document.

3. On page 7, **insert an endnote immediately after the text "geographic reach."**

   a. **Find the text "geographic reach."**

   b. **Place the insertion point immediately after "reach."**

   c. **In the Footnote And Endnote dialog box, select Endnotes and click Insert.**

   d. **In the Endnote area, type** *We cover 8 states*.

   e. **Position the I-beam over the reference mark and double-click on it** to return to the document text.

4. **What page of the document does the endnote appear on?**

Browse By Footnote or Endnote

If you have a very long document that contains many footnotes or endnotes, and you're looking for a specific footnote, but you are not sure exactly what text is in the bookmark or where it is in the document, you can use the Select Browse Object menu (below the Vertical scroll bar) to browse through your document moving from footnote to footnote (or endnote to endnote) when you click the Next and Previous buttons.

DISCOVERY ACTIVITY 3-3

Changing an Endnote to a Footnote

Scenario:

You decided to check back through your document and see where your footnotes are, because you think the endnote you just inserted should really be a footnote. After reviewing the two footnotes in the document, you decide that your endnote should really be a footnote, so you convert it and save the document as My Stockholder Report.

1. **Browse to and review each footnote in the document.**

2. **Change the endnote to a footnote.**

TOPIC C

Add Captions

In addition to referencing the text in your document, you might also want to refer to graphics, tables, or equations. In this topic, you'll add captions to figures so that you can more easily refer to them in your document.

In manuals or other long documents, sometimes the figures, tables, and equations are numbered so that readers know exactly which figure, table, or equation is being referred to in the text. You can create your own captions, but then if you have a long document, or if you add additional objects you want to refer to, you have to keep track of what number you're on and occasionally renumber captions. Fortunately, you can use Word's built-in figure, table, and equation captions to automatically create and number captions.

Insert Figure Captions

Procedure Reference: Add Captions to Figures

Using Word's Caption command, you can add captions to the graphics, tables, and equations in your documents. To add captions to figures:

1. Select the item (figure, table, or equation) that needs a caption.

2. Choose Insert→Reference→Caption to open the Caption dialog box.

3. In the Caption text box, enter a caption for the item. You can't change the number of the item, because Word numbers automatically.

4. From the Label drop-down list, select the type of item you are creating a caption for. For example, select Figure to insert the word "Figure" before the item number.

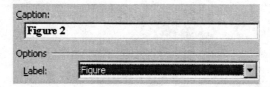

5. From the Position drop-down menu, select a position for the caption. Word can place the caption either above or below the selected item.

6. Click OK.

If you delete graphics, tables, or equations that have captions, you need to update the numbering for the captions following the one(s) you deleted. To update captions for the entire document:

1. Select the document.

2. Press [Alt][F9].

ACTIVITY 3-4

Adding Captions to Figures

Setup:

My Stockholder Report.doc is open.

Scenario:

There are two figures in your stockholder report that you need to refer to. You started by just telling the reader to look at the figure below; however, you quickly realized that the figure might not actually wind up below the text. It might be on the next page. So, you decide to add a caption to each of the figures in the document. You want the figure to automatically number and you want text explaining that the first figure is a diagram of the Burke Properties department strategy and the second figure shows the Relocation Services management team. When you're finished, save the file and close the file.

What You Do	How You Do It
1. On the line below the organization chart, **insert a figure caption**.	a. **Place the insertion point on the blank line below the organization chart on page 5.**
	b. **Choose Insert→Reference→Caption to open the Caption dialog box.**
	c. **In the Caption text box, type** *:Relocation Services Management Team*.
	d. **If necessary, in the Options section, select Figure from the Label drop-down list.**
	e. **Click OK.**

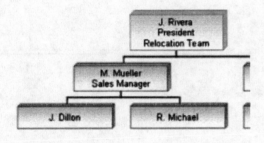

Figure·1:·Relocation·Services·Management·Team¶

2. On the blank line below the first graphic in the document, **insert a caption.**

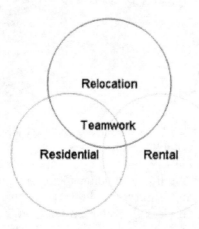

Figure·1·:·Burke·Properties·Department·Strategy¶

a. **Place the insertion point on the blank line beneath the graphic on page 4.**

b. **Open the Caption dialog box**(choose Insert→Reference→Caption).

c. **Enter the figure caption** *:Burke Properties Department Strategy* **and click OK.**

3. **How did the figure number for the organization chart change?**

Save and close the file.

TOPIC D

Create Cross-References

You know how to insert figure captions and footnotes and endnotes. Another way that you can refer to document information is with a cross-reference. In this topic, you'll create cross-references.

Suppose you create a document that contains several figures with captions to which you refer in the text. Then, when you review your work, you decide that you need to add a new figure at the beginning of the document. If you haven't used cross-references to refer to the figures in your document text, you'll have to keep track of what figure number you're on and remember to change it when you add another figure.

Cross-references

Definition:

A *cross-reference* is a pointer in a document that refers to specific information in the same document or in another document. In Word, you can create cross-references for numbered items, headings, bookmarks, footnotes, endnotes, equations, figures, and tables.

Example:

Figure 3-2 shows an example of a cross-reference in a document.

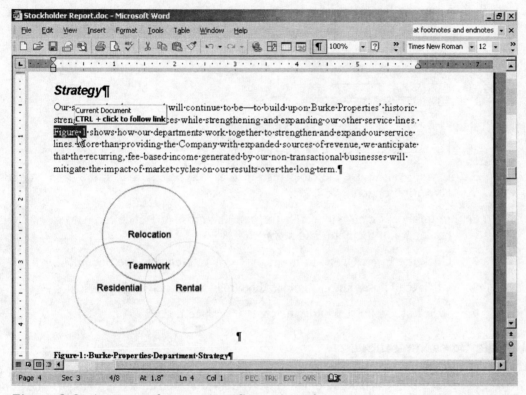

Figure 3-2: *A cross-reference to a figure in a document.*

Create a Cross-reference

Procedure Reference: Create a Cross-reference

To create a cross-reference:

1. In the document, type the cross-reference text. For example, for a figure, you might type "See" before you insert the cross-reference.

2. Choose Insert→Reference→Cross-Reference to open the Cross-Reference dialog box.

3. In the Reference Type drop-down list, select what the cross-reference refers to.

4. From the Insert Reference To drop-down list, select what the cross-reference refers to. For example, in the case of a figure, you have these options:

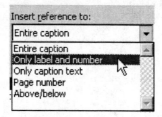

5. If you want to use the cross-reference as a hyperlink, check the Insert As Hyperlink option.

6. In the For Which box, select the item the cross-reference refers to (a caption, a bookmark, a footnote, and so on).

7. Click the Insert button to insert the cross-reference in the document.

8. Click the Close button to close the Cross-Reference dialog box.

9. If necessary, finish typing the cross-reference text.

Update Cross-References

If you add or delete pages or graphics from your document, the numbers in your cross-references don't update automatically. You need to update them yourself. The good news is you can update them all at the same time. To do so, select the entire document and press [F9]. Word will go through the document and automatically update all cross-references (as well as any other fields in the document).

ACTIVITY 3-5

Creating a Cross-reference to a Figure

Data Files:

- Cross-reference.doc

Scenario:

Each of the figures in your Stockholder report is numbered and has a caption. Now, in your document text, you need to refer readers to the figures. You thought you might just type the text "see figure 1," but a co-worker mentioned that you can create a cross-reference that will update automatically if you move the figure or add additional figures before it. This sounds like a good idea, so you decide to add an appropriate cross-reference to each figure within the document text. When you're finished, save the file as My Cross-Reference.doc and close the file.

What You Do	How You Do It
1. At the beginning of the second sentence in the Strategy section of the Cross-reference document, **insert a cross-reference to Figure 1.**	a. **Open Cross-reference.doc and find the Strategy heading.** (The Strategy heading is at the bottom of page 3.)
	b. **Place the insertion point before the word "shows" in the second sentence under the Strategy heading.**

*Strate

Our·stra
strength
shows·l

	c. **Choose Insert→Reference→Cross-reference** to open the Cross-reference dialog box.
	d. From the Reference Type drop-down list, **select Figure.**
	e. From the Insert Reference To drop-down list, **select Only Label And Number.**
	f. **Uncheck Insert As Hyperlink.**
	g. If necessary, in the For Which Caption box, **select Figure 1.**
	h. **Click Insert and then click Close** to insert the cross-reference in the document and close the Cross-reference dialog box.
	i. **Add a space between the cross-reference and the text.**

2. In the New Relocation Team section, insert a cross-reference in the second sentence that tells readers to see Figure 2.

*New·Relocation·Team¶

Because·revenue·generated·by·relocatio Current Document
create·a·new·team·that·will·focus·solely CTRL + click to follow link
Services·management·team·(see·Figure·2)·are·all·strong·manage
record·of·sales·and·customer·service. We·expect·to·see·revenues
year·thanks·to·their·focus·and·experience.¶

J. Rivera
President
Relocation Team

a. Find the "New Relocation Team" heading.

b. Place the insertion point between "team" and "are" in the second sentence and type *(see* and then press [Spacebar].

c. Open the Cross-Reference dialog box and insert a hyperlink reference to Figure 2.

d. Close the Cross-Reference dialog box and type *)* to complete the cross-reference.

e. Save the document as *My Cross-Reference.doc* and close the file.

Lesson 3 Follow-up

If you take the time to research and write a long report, you want to make sure that everyone who reads the report clearly understands what you're referring to and who your sources are. In this lesson, you learned how to create references so that important information in your documents doesn't get lost.

1. Which types of document references are you most likely to use in your documents? Why?

2. Is it important for you to reference information in the documents you create? Why or why not?

NOTES

LESSON 4

Preparing a Document for Publication

Lesson Time
50 minutes to 60 minutes

Lesson Objectives:

In this lesson, you will prepare a document for publication.

You will:

• Set gutter and mirror margins for a document.

• Create different first page and even and odd headers and footers.

• Create a table of contents for a document.

• Generate an index for a document.

• Create a master document that contains at least three subdocuments.

Introduction

If you use Microsoft Word to create long documents, then you know that preparing to print a document involves a lot of finishing work. In this lesson, you'll walk through the process for preparing a long document for publication.

Everyone in the company was complaining because there wasn't one source for information on the company benefits. So, you took the time to put together a 200-page book listing and explaining the company benefits. It was time-consuming creating that manual. After you finished, everyone still complained that they didn't know what the company benefits were. Why? Because even though you compiled the benefits into one document, you didn't include a table of contents, an index, or headers and footers that helped people locate the information they needed. It's important to make sure that your documents are ready for publication and that they include all of the things readers need so that they don't get lost in the document.

TOPIC A

Set Book Margins

You know how to set standard margins for your documents. If you have a document, such as a report, that you plan to bind, you'll want to customize the margins. In this topic, you'll learn how to set margins for bound documents.

You have a document that is several chapters long and you plan to print that document and distribute it to co-workers. If you don't set the appropriate margins for your document, you're likely to lose part of the text when you have the document bound. To make sure this doesn't happen, you need to change the margin settings.

Mirror Margins

As you prepare your long documents for publication, you may need to change the margin settings for your documents. You might choose to set mirror margins and gutter margins for your documents.

Definition:

> *Mirror margins* is a Word feature, that when active, allows you to set the inside and outside margins for the right page of a document while simultaneously creating a mirror image of those margin settings on the left page. This means that the inside and outside margins on the left page will be the same as the inside and outside margins on the right page.

Example:

> If you're preparing a document for double-sided printing—for example, the company newsletter—you might want to consider using mirror margins.

Gutter Margins

When you bind a document, you use space on the inside edge of the paper. You need to allow for extra room in the margin settings; otherwise, the binding may pierce or overlap the text.

Definition:

A *gutter margin* is space that is added to the inside margin of a page so that the text isn't obscured by the binding method.

Example:

If the inside margin of a page is 1 inch, adding a gutter margin of 0.5 inches will make the total inside margin 1.5 inches, giving you an extra half-inch of margin space for the book binding.

Figure 4-1 shows an example of a document in which mirror margins of 1 inch and a 0.75-inch gutter have been set. Notice that the left margin of page 1 mirrors the right margin on page 2. The inside margins (right margin on page 1 and the left margin on page 2) are .75-inches larger than the outside margins to allow room for binding the document without obscuring the text.

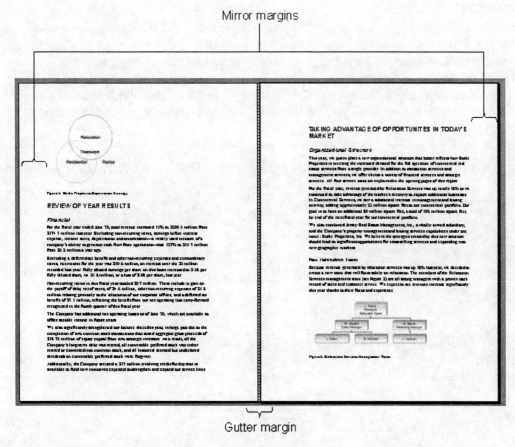

Figure 4-1: *A document with 1-inch mirror margins and a 0.75-inch gutter.*

Set Gutter and Mirror Margins

Procedure Reference: Set Mirror and Gutter Margins

To set mirror and gutter margins:

1. Choose File→Page Setup and display the Margins tab.

2. From the Pages drop-down list, select Mirror Margins.

3. Set the inside and outside margins for the document. Use the Preview area to see how your changes will affect the document.

4. In the Gutter text box, set the gutter measurement based on how much space the binding will take.

5. Click OK.

DISCOVERY ACTIVITY 4-1

Setting Book Margins for the Document

Data Files:

* Preparing Documents.doc

Scenario:

You're just about finished with your Stockholder report. Last year, the report was included in a folder handed out to stockholders at the annual meeting. This year, management decided it would be a nice touch to have the report spiral-bound so that all the pages will stay together. The spiral binding will take at least a half-inch of space on the inside edge of the paper. To ensure that the margins for the left and right pages are the same and that the document text is not obscured by the binding, you decide to set mirror margins and a gutter margin.

1. In Preparing Documents.doc, **set 1-inch mirror margins and a 0.75-inch gutter margin.**

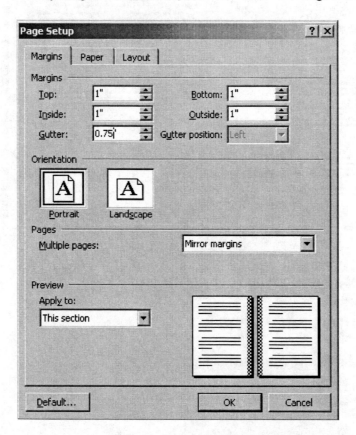

2. Using Figure 4-1 as a guide, **check the margins in Print Preview.**

    In Print Layout view, **save the document as** *My Preparing Documents.*

TOPIC B

Create Custom Headers and Footers

Once you have set the margins for a document you are planning to bind, it's time to turn your attention to the headers and footers for that document. You know how to create standard headers and footers. In this topic, you will customize those standard headers and footers so that you have a different header and footer for even and odd pages and no header or footer on the cover page of your document.

Pick up any book on your bookshelf. Chances are, it has a different header or footer for left- and right-side pages. One way to make your long documents look more professional, like the books on your bookshelf, is to create different headers and footers for the left and right pages of your document.

Create Odd and Even Headers and Footers

Procedure Reference: Create a Different First Page and Odd and Even Headers and Footers

To create a different first page and odd and even headers and footers:

1. Place the insertion point at the top of the document.

2. Choose View→Header And Footer to display the Header And Footer toolbar.

3. Click the Page Setup button 📖 .

4. On the Layout tab in the Page Setup dialog box, check the Different Odd And Even and the Different First Page options.

5. Click OK.

6. If you want a header and footer on the first page of the document, enter the header and footer elements for the first page.

7. Click the Show Next button to move to the even-page header or footer.

8. Enter the header and footer elements for the even pages and click the Show Next button.

9. Enter the header and footer elements for the odd pages.

10. Close the Header And Footer toolbar.

DISCOVERY ACTIVITY 4-2

Creating Different Footers for the Odd and Even Pages in a Document

Setup:

My Preparing Documents.doc is open.

Scenario:

You're working on the Stockholder report and you decide that since you've set beautiful custom margins, you should set custom footers to go with those margins. You have a book on your desk that displays the name of the document followed by the page number at the outside margin of each page. You decide that this would work for your report, too. In addition, you don't want the footer to appear on the first page of the report because that is going to hold the table of contents.

1. In My Preparing Documents.doc, **set up your footer so that it doesn't appear on the first page of your document and so that you can create a different footer for even and odd pages.**

2. For the even pages in your document, **create the footer shown here.**

3. For the odd pages in your document, **create the footer shown here.** When you're finished, **save and close the document.**

TOPIC C

Compile a Table of Contents

Once you've created and formatted your document text, you're ready to start adding the information that will make your document more useful. In this topic, you will compile a table of contents for your document.

If you've ever spent time flipping through a reference book looking for a specific topic, you know the importance of including a table of contents in a document that contains many topics. A table of contents helps your readers quickly find the section they are looking for in your document.

Create a Table of Contents

When you create a table of contents, you begin by deciding what you should put in the table of contents. Then, once you have decided what to include, you apply styles to the headings in your document. Finally, you can generate your table of contents based on the heading styles in the document.

Procedure Reference: Create a Table of Contents

To create a Table Of Contents (TOC) for your document:

1. In the document, place the insertion point where you want to generate the table of contents.

2. Choose Insert→Reference→Index And Tables.

3. Display the Table Of Contents tab.

4. From the Formats drop-down list, select a design for your table of contents. You can use the Print Preview box to see what your design looks like.

5. In the Show Levels text box, set the number of levels for your table of contents.

   The levels are based on heading styles in your document. Level 1 is based on the Heading 1 style, level 2 is based on the Heading 2 style, and so on.

6. From the Tab Leader drop-down list, select a tab leader—the character that appears between the heading reference and the page number in a TOC.

7. Click OK. Word goes through the document and compiles the headings into a table of contents at the location of the insertion point.

Once you generate your table of contents, it becomes an easy way to navigate through your document. Each entry in the table of contents acts as a hyperlink. If you [Ctrl]-click on an entry, Word jumps to that spot in the document.

ACTIVITY 4-3

Creating a Table of Contents

Data Files:

- Final Stockholder Report.doc

Scenario:

You've almost completed a report for Burke Properties stockholders. Last year, people complained that it wasn't easy to find information in the report, so this year, you've decided to include a table of contents at the beginning of the document. The document has several different sections that are formatted with Word's default heading styles so you can have Word compile a one-level table of contents for you. When you're finished, you decide to save your file as My Final Stockholders Report.

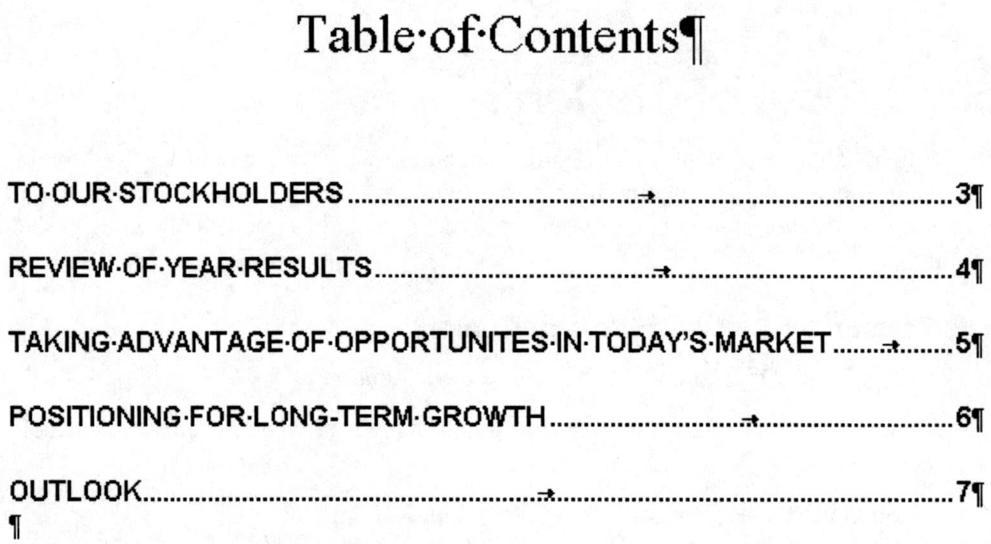
Table·of·Contents¶

TO·OUR·STOCKHOLDERS .... 3¶
REVIEW·OF·YEAR·RESULTS .... 4¶
TAKING·ADVANTAGE·OF·OPPORTUNITES·IN·TODAY'S·MARKET .... 5¶
POSITIONING·FOR·LONG-TERM·GROWTH .... 6¶
OUTLOOK .... 7¶
¶

Figure 4-2: *The table of contents.*

What You Do	How You Do It
1. In Final Stockholder Report.doc, using Figure 4-2 as a guide, **compile a one-level table of contents on the second page of the document.**	a. In Final Stockholder Report.doc, **place the insertion point on the first blank line on the Table Of Contents page.**
	b. **Choose Insert→Reference→Index And Tables.**
	c. If necessary, **display the Table Of Contents tab.**
	d. From the Formats drop-down list, **select Classic.**
	e. From the Tab Leader drop-down list, **select the first leader option.**

	f. In the Show Levels text box, **enter 1 to create a one-level table of contents.**
	g. **Click OK.**
	h. **Save the file as *My Final Stockholder Report*.**

Update a Table of Contents

As you create your documents, you continuously add and remove content. Even once you think the document is final, there is likely to be some minor change that you need to make. Even minor changes can affect your table of contents. Fortunately, you can update your table of contents. To do so:

1. Right-click on the existing table of contents and select Update Field from the shortcut menu.

2. From the Update Table Of Contents dialog box, select either Update Page Numbers Only if you only added text, or Update Entire Table if you've added new headings to your document.

3. Click OK.

ACTIVITY 4-4

Updating and Modifying a Table of Contents

Data Files:

* Management Team.doc

Setup:

My Final Stockholder Report is open.

Scenario:

You thought your Stockholder report was complete, so you generated a table of contents; however, you've been asked to add a new section on Management just before the Outlook heading. Your manager gave you a document called Management Team that contains all the text you need to add to the report. You can just insert the file and you won't have to worry about typing; however, you'll also need to update the table of contents because the new text changes the page numbers. When you're finished, don't forget to save the file.

What You Do	How You Do It
1. Before the Outlook section, **insert the file Management Team.doc .**	a. **Point to the last entry in the table of contents, Outlook. Press [Ctrl] and click once** to jump to the Outlook section of the document.
	b. **Choose Insert→File** to open the Insert File dialog box.
	c. In the My Documents folder, **double-click on Management Team.doc** to insert the file into the document before the Outlook heading.
2. **Update the entire table of contents and save the file.**	a. **Go to page 1.**
	b. **Right-click on the table of contents** to display the shortcut menu.
	c. **Choose Update Field.**
	d. In the Update Table Of Contents dialog box, **select Update Entire Table and click OK.**
	e. **Save the file.**

Update Table of Contents ? X

Word is updating the table of contents. Select one of the following options:

○ Update page numbers only
◉ Update entire table

OK   Cancel

3. How has the table of contents changed?

Modify a Table of Contents

If you don't like the way your table of contents looks, perhaps you want to change its format or add a few more levels of detail. You can always modify a table of contents. To do so:

1. Choose Insert→Reference→Index And Tables.

2. Change the settings on the Table Of Contents tab.

3. Click OK to close the dialog box.

4. Click Yes to replace the selected table of contents.

ACTIVITY 4-5

Changing the Style and Levels for the Table of Contents

Setup:

My Final Stockholder Report.doc is open.

Scenario:

Your manager passed the Stockholder report on to her manager, and she doesn't think the table of contents is useful enough the way it is. There isn't enough detail and she also isn't sure she likes the format you used for the table of contents. She would like you to try a different level and format to see if the table of contents looks a little better and is more useful. After you make the changes, save the file.

Table·of·Contents¶

Figure 4-3: *The table of contents with three levels and the Formal format applied.*

What You Do	How You Do It
1. Using Figure 4-3 as a guide, **modify the table of contents.**	a. **Choose Insert→Reference→Index And Tables.**
	b. On the Table Of Contents tab, from the Formats drop-down list, **select Formal.**
	c. In the Show Levels box, **set the number of levels for the table of contents to 3.**
	d. **Click OK.**
	e. **Click OK** to replace the existing table of contents.
	f. **Save the file.**

TOPIC D

Index the Document

You know how to create a table of contents for your document, but people also like to look up specific terms in the back of the book and find out where they're covered in the book. In this topic, you'll create an index for your document.

No manual or long report is complete without an index that readers can refer to when they want to look up information. Next to the table of contents, the easiest way to find anything in a long document is to look in the index.

An Index Defined

Definition:

An *index* is an alphabetical guide to words, phrases, and concepts in your documents. It appears at the end of the document and indicates the page on which each word, phrase, or concept is located, so you can quickly find that information.

As with the table of contents, Word will generate an index for you based on index entries marked in your document. There are two ways you can mark index entries in your documents. You can mark them one at a time in the Mark Index Entry dialog box, or you can create a *concordance file* —a file containing the words you want Word to search for and mark in your document—and use that file to mark your index entries all at once.

Example:

Figure 4-4 shows a sample index created using a concordance file.

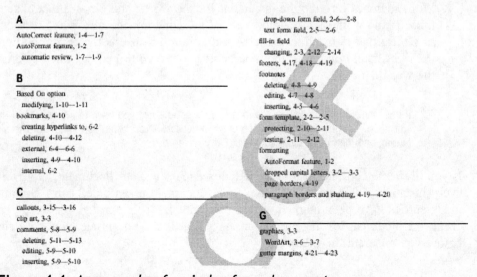

INDEX

A
AutoCorrect feature, 1-4—1-7
AutoFormat feature, 1-2
  automatic review, 1-7—1-9

B
Based On option
  modifying, 1-10—1-11
bookmarks, 4-10
  creating hyperlinks to, 6-2
  deleting, 4-10—4-12
  external, 6-4—6-6
  inserting, 4-9—4-10
  internal, 6-2

C
callouts, 3-15—3-16
clip art, 3-3
comments, 5-8—5-9
  deleting, 5-11—5-13
  editing, 5-9—5-10
  inserting, 5-9—5-10

drop-down form field, 2-6—2-8
  text form field, 2-5—2-6
fill-in field
  changing, 2-3, 2-12—2-14
footers, 4-17, 4-18—4-19
footnotes
  deleting, 4-8—4-9
  editing, 4-7—4-8
  inserting, 4-5—4-6
form template, 2-2—2-5
  protecting, 2-10—2-11
  testing, 2-11—2-12
formatting
  AutoFormat feature, 1-2
  dropped capital letters, 3-2—3-3
  page borders, 4-19
  paragraph borders and shading, 4-19—4-20

G
graphics, 3-3
  WordArt, 3-6—3-7
gutter margins, 4-21—4-23

Figure 4-4: *An example of an index for a document.*

Create a Condordance File

Procedure Reference: Create a Concordance File

Before you can use a concordance file to mark index entries in a document, you have to create the concordance file. To create a concordance file:

1. In a new blank document, insert a two-column table. It doesn't matter how many rows.

2. In the first column of the table, enter the words you want Word to search for and mark as index entries.

   For example, if you want Word to search the document for the text"Future Objectives," you would enter that in a cell in the left-hand column of the table.

3. In the second column, enter the words as you want them to appear in the index. You can use a colon to indicate a sub-entry.

   If you want "Future Objectives" referenced in the index with "Future" appearing as a sub-entry for "Objectives," you would type "Objectives: Future" in the right-hand column of the table.

4. Save the file.

Mark the Index

Procedure Reference: Use a Concordance File to Mark an Index

By far the quickest way to mark index entries is to use a concordance file to mark the index.

1. In the document you want to index, choose Insert→Reference→Index And Tables.

2. On the Index tab, click the AutoMark button.

3. In the Open Index AutoMark File dialog box, double-click on the concordance file you want to use.

   Word searches through the document for the words and phrases that exactly match those found in the left-hand column of the concordance file. When it finds a word or phrase that is listed in the left-hand column, it inserts the corresponding text in the right-hand column as the index entry, along with the page number on which the word is found.

 If you want to mark index entries manually, select the text you want to index; press [Alt][Shift]X; edit the main entry and create a sub-entry, if necessary; click the Mark button or the Mark All button; and then close the Mark Index Entry dialog box.

If you use a concordance file to mark index entries in your document, Word marks every instance of the word or phrase in the document as an index entry. So, after the index entries have been marked, take a few minutes to go through the document and check the index entries. If you find an entry that isn't appropriate, you can delete it before you generate the index.

ACTIVITY 4-6

Using a Concordance File to Automatically Mark Index Entries in a Document

Data Files:

- Burke Concordance.doc

Setup:

My Final Stockholder Report.doc is open.

Scenario:

You're ready to mark index terms in your document. You don't have a lot of time, so you've decided to use a concordance file and have Word mark all of your terms for you. You've started gathering all the terms you want in a file called Burke Concordance. First you need to add a few more terms to the concordance file. You want to make sure you index the term "net income" and index the term "relocation" as a sub-entry for services. When you're finished with the concordance file, you save it as My Burke Concordance and then close it. Then, you'll use the concordance file to mark the index terms in your document. When you're finished, the marked index entries should appear in your document.

What You Do	How You Do It
1. In a new row at the end of the Burke Concordance.doc file, **create an index entry for "net income."**	a. **Add a new row to the end of the table.**
	b. In the first cell in the new row, **type** *net income*.
	c. In the second cell in the new row, **type** *net income*.
2. In a new row at the end of the table, **mark the text "relocation services" so that "relocation" appears as a sub-entry for "services."**	a. **Add a new row to the end of the table.**
	b. In the first cell in the new row, **type** *relocation services*.
	c. In the second cell in the new row, **type** *services: relocation*.
	d. **Save the file as** *My Burke Concordance*.
	e. **Close the file.**

3. In My Final Stockholder Report.doc , use the My Burke Concordance file to mark index entries.

    a. **Choose Insert→Reference→Index And Tables.**

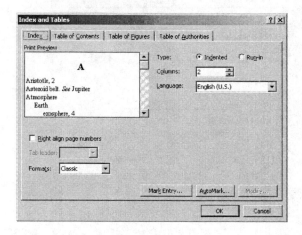

    b. **Display the Index tab.**

    c. **Click the AutoMark button** to display the Open Index AutoMark File dialog box.

    d. **Select My Burke Concordance.doc.**

    e. **Click Open.**

4. **Scroll through the document and find the index entries.**

    How can you tell Word has marked the index entries in the document?

    Will these index entries print in the document? Why or why not?

Generate an Index

Procedure Reference: Generate an Index

Once you've marked index entries in your document, generating the index is easy. To generate an index:

1. At the end of the document, create and format a heading for the Index.

2. Place the insertion point where you want to generate the index.

3. Choose Insert→Reference→Index And Tables and display the Index tab, if necessary.

4. From the Formats list box, select an index style.

5. Click OK. Word generates the index at the location of the insertion point.

ACTIVITY 4-7

Generating an Index

Setup:
My Final Stockholder Report.doc is open.

Scenario:
All of the terms you want to appear in your index are marked in your document. Now it's time to generate the index. You want your index to be two columns, Modern style, and right-aligned with a dot leader. When you're finished, it should look like the one shown in Figure 4-5.

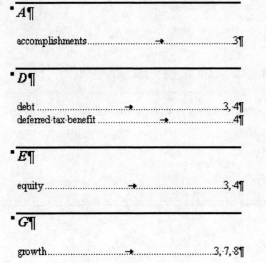

Figure 4-5: *The completed index.*

LESSON 4

What You Do	How You Do It
1. Using Figure 4-5 as a guide, below the Index heading, **generate a right-aligned index.**	a. On the line below the Index heading, **choose Insert→Reference→Index And Tables.**
	b. If necessary, **display the Index tab.**
	c. If necessary, **set the number of columns to 2.**
	d. If necessary, from the Type options, **select the Indented option.**
	e. From the Formats list box, **select Modern.**
	f. **Check the Right Align Page Numbers option.**
	g. From the Tab Leader box, **select a dot leader.**

	h. **Click OK** to generate the index.

2. **How does the relocation services entry you created in the concordance file appear in the index?**

   Save and close the file.

TOPIC E

Create a Master Document

If you need to create one report that will be longer than 50 pages and include documents written by several different people, you might want to create a container for the several different documents. In this topic, you'll create a master document that consists of several subdocuments.

It's your job to organize and distribute the company newsletter. The CEO wrote a letter that you want to include on the first page. The sales force blew away their numbers last quarter and they want to share that with the rest of the company, and the Marketing department wants to introduce the new company logo and several new products for the next quarter. You could write all of that information in one document yourself, but if you have many different people contributing to the document, you can save time by creating a master document that strings together separate documents created by each department that wants to contribute to the newsletter.

Master Document and Subdocuments

Definition:

A *master document* is a container that holds text and links to a series of related documents called subdocuments. You can use the master document to chunk a large document into smaller, more manageable pieces—the subdocuments. Because they are smaller, the subdocuments may be easier to work in. Additionally, it may be easier for you to rearrange your document by moving subdocuments within the master document.

Because your subdocuments exist outside of the master document, you can work in either the master document, or one of the subdocuments, and the work you do in one will appear in both places.

Example:

In Figure 4-6, you see an example of an existing document that was converted into a master document.

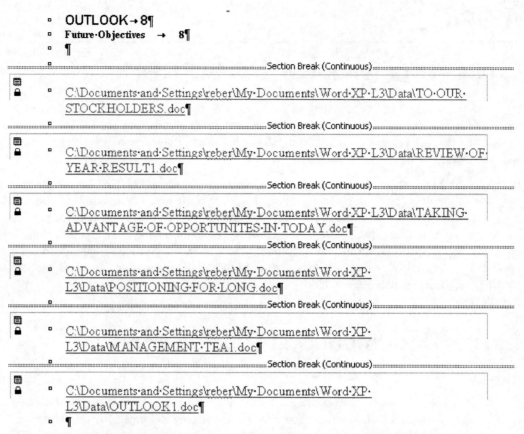

Figure 4-6: *An existing document converted to a master document.*

Advantages and Disadvantages

If you think you might like to use master documents to create your long documents, there are several advantages and disadvantages you should consider before you decide to create a master document.

Advantages include:

- Manageability. By storing a master document in a central location (on a network or Web server), several people can be working on its individual subdocuments simultaneously.

- Flexibility. Individual subdocuments can be opened outside the master document, making them easier and faster to edit. Additionally, you can drag and drop subdocuments in the master document's Outline view to achieve the arrangement you want.

- Consistency. The master document's template overrides those of the subdocuments, ensuring consistent formatting throughout the long document.

Disadvantages include:

- Slow Performance. The master document sometimes uses more computer memory, especially if you have graphics, sound files, or other memory-intensive items in the document.

- Lost Documents. If you move the master document or subdocuments, Word will not be able to find them.

Create a Master Document

There are two ways you can create a master document: from scratch and from an existing document.

Procedure Reference: Create from Scratch

You might want to create a master document from scratch if you have several documents already created that you want to combine into one larger document. For example, suppose it's your job to put together a report that includes contributions from several team members. In that case, you might receive a file from each member of the team and use a master document to compile them into your final report.

To create a master document from scratch:

1. Open a new blank document (which will become your master document) and switch to Outline view.

2. Enter any text you want to store in the master document. For example, you might want to store the title page, the table of contents and the index headings in the master document.

3. If necessary, display the Outlining toolbar.

4. Click the Master Document View button ⊡ .

5. Use the Insert Subdocument button ⊟ on the Outlining toolbar to add subdocuments to your master document.

6. Save the master document.

Procedure Reference: Create from an Existing Document

If you already have a long document that you want to turn into a master document, you can easily do so. For example, suppose you create a document that is fifty pages long and has six chapters. Instead of working with the 50 pages as one document, you may find it easier to turn the existing document into a master document and make each of the chapters a subdocument. To turn an existing document into a master document:

1. Open the existing long document and switch to Outline view.

2. If necessary, click the Master Document View button.

3. Select the text you want to convert to a subdocument.

4. Click the Create Subdocument button on the Outlining toolbar.

5. Save the master document. When you do so, Word also saves the text you designated as a subdocument as a separate file in the same folder as the master document.

Regardless of the method you use to create a master document, each subdocument has a corresponding subdocument icon and is enclosed in a box with a section break before it.

Remove Sub-documents

As you build your master document, you may decide that a particular subdocument should become part of the master document text. To make a subdocument part of the master document text, you'll need to remove its subdocument designation. To do so:

1. Click on the subdocument icon to select the subdocument.

2.   Click the Remove Subdocument button .

 If you want to delete a subdocument from the master document entirely, press [Delete] instead of clicking the Remove Subdocument button.

ACTIVITY 4-8

Creating a Master Document

Data Files:

- Company History.doc
- Feedback.doc
- Services.doc
- Merchandise.doc

Scenario:

You're a consultant for the company Books & Beyond. They want you to put together a booklet that will be available online. Each of the different departments put together a section of the booklet and saved it as a document. You just need to combine them into one document that starts with the company history, followed by the merchandise, services, and feedback sections. When you're finished, save the document as My Master Document.

What You Do	How You Do It
1. In a new blank document, **create a heading for the booklet.** This heading is text that is stored in the master document.	a. **Click the New Blank Document button.**
	b. **Type** *All About* **and format it as centered, 36 pt., and Arial.**
All·About¶ **Books·&·Beyond¶**	c. **On the next line, type** *Books & Beyond* **and format it as centered, 48 pt., bold, and Arial.**
	d. **After the heading, create a new blank line.**
2. In Outline view, **insert the first subdocument.**	a. **Switch to Outline view. (Choose View→ Outline.)**
	b. **Click the Insert Subdocument button.**
	c. **In the Insert Subdocument dialog box, double-click on Company History.doc.**

3. **Scroll through and look at the document.**

How does this document look different from the documents you usually work on?

···········Section Break (Next Page)···········

✧ What·Is·Books·&·Beyond?¶

☐ Some·people·say·it·is·a·bookstore.·Some·call·it·a·music·shop,·while·others·think·of· it·as·a·great·place·to·meet·and·have·refreshments.·Books·&·Beyond·has·become·a· unique·phenomenon·that·not·only·offers·this·area's·largest·selection·of·sale·books,· but·has·also·branched·into·the·world·of·music,·with·an·inventory·of·CDs·and·tapes· ranging·from·New·Age·to·Alternative·Rock·and·everything·in·between.·What· makes·us·different·is·our·atmosphere.·We·encourage·our·visitors·to·relax·with·a· book·in·one·of·our·quiet·rooms,·or·take·some·reading·material·into·our·Coffee·and· Juice·Bar·to·read·while·snacking.¶

☐ Have·you·ever·wanted·to·spend·some·quiet·time·away·from·home?·Many·of·us· find·that·solitude·buried·in·the·pages·of·a·good·book·or·lost·in·the·sounds·of· musical·instruments.·Maybe·you·want·to·visit·with·a·friend·over·a·cup·of· cappuccino·or·a·fresh-squeezed·juice·blend,·or·just·take·a·break·from·the·shopping· mall·and·treat·yourself·to·a·scrumptious·dessert.·You·can·do·all·those·things·at· Books·&·Beyond.¶

···········Section Break (Continuous)···········

4. **Insert the rest of the subdocuments into the master document. When you're finished, save the file as My Master Document.**

a. **Place the insertion point at the end of the document and click the Insert Subdocument button** 🖻 **.**

b. **Double-click on Merchandise.doc to add it to the master document following the Company History section.**

c. **Click the Insert Subdocument button and double-click on Services.doc to add it to the master document following the Merchandise subdocument.**

d. **Click the Insert Subdocument button and double-click on Feedback.doc to add it to the master document.**

e. **Save the file as *My Master Document*.**

5. **Open the Company History.doc subdocument in a new Word window.**

a. **Click the Collapse Subdocuments button** . Word displays the subdocuments as links.

b. **Press [Ctrl] and click on the Company History link.** It opens in a new Microsoft Word window.

    You can also double-click on the subdocument icon to open a subdocument in its own window.

c. **Close the file.**

6. **Expand the subdocuments and close the file.**

a. **Click the Expand Subdocuments button** .

b. **Close the file.**

Lesson 4 Follow-up

When you create reference materials, such as training manuals or long reports, it is important to make sure that readers can find the section they need without having to wade through an entire document. In this lesson, you learned how to combine several documents into one, how to change the margins and set headers and footers for that long document, and how to create a table of contents and index to make it easier for readers to use the document as reference material.

1. **What types of long documents are you likely to create for your job?**

2. **How can the techniques you learned in this lesson make your long documents easier to use?**

LESSON 5
Revising Documents

Lesson Time
40 minutes to 50 minutes

Lesson Objectives:

In this lesson, you will revise documents based on feedback provided by other users.

You will:

- Create multiple versions of a document.
- Distribute a document for review.
- Track changes to a document.
- Review changes to a document.

Introduction

You know how to create and work with documents on your own, and now it's time to learn how to work with documents with other Word users. In this lesson, you will walk through the process of collaborating on Word documents.

Imagine that you have a document that you would like some of your co-workers to look at and give you feedback on. You could take the document to each one of them individually and write down their suggestions, but that would be time-consuming, and what if they made suggestions that you didn't like? If you're talking to them, you have to be diplomatic. To make incorporating edits a little easier, consider using Word's collaboration tools.

TOPIC A

Create Document Versions

After you edit a document, you generally save the changes by either overwriting the existing document (Save) or saving the changed document with a new file name (Save As). Saving over an existing document doesn't create a new file, but you have no way of going back to the original document if you need. Saving the changed document with a new name keeps the original file intact, but it also creates a new file on your hard drive. In this topic, you'll learn how to save the current state of your document without saving it as a new file or overwriting the existing document by creating document versions.

Many times when you create a document, you create a rough draft first and then make changes or fill in the missing pieces. As your document changes, you may find that you liked an earlier draft of your document. To find that earlier draft, you may have to search through many documents on your hard drive. And, if you've updated the file, you may have lost that earlier draft entirely. Unless you save versions of your document, going back to an earlier draft of your document isn't always as easy as it sounds.

Create Different Versions of a Document

Procedure Reference: Save a Version of a Document

To save a version of your document:

1. If necessary, save the original document. You can't save versions of a document until you first save the document.

2. Choose File→Versions.

3. Click the Save Now button to open the Save Version dialog box.

4. In the Comments On Version text box, type any comments about the version you're saving. For example, you might want to document the changes you've made.

5. Click OK. The version you just created appears in the Existing Versions list.

6. If necessary, close the Versions dialog box.

The Versions Dialog Box

Table 5-1 and Figure 5-1 describe and display the components of the Versions dialog box.

Table 5-1: *The Versions Dialog Box Options*

Option	Description
Save Now	Saves the current state of the document as a version.
Existing Versions	Lists the existing versions of the document. You can select an existing version and open it, delete it, or display comments for it.
Automatically Save A Version On Close	Automatically saves a version of your document each time you close it. If you select this option, you cannot enter any comments to remind you what the version is.

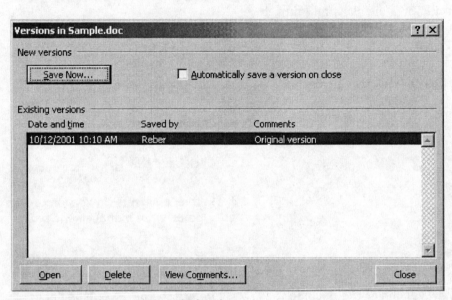

Figure 5-1: *The Versions dialog box.*

ACTIVITY 5-1

Creating More than One Version of a Document

Data Files:

- Revise Management.doc

Scenario:

The Management section of your Stockholder report is going to change. There's talk that the Relocation Team is going to be split out as a separate company, so you want to remove that section from the document; however, you know that talk is cheap and the new company might not become a reality, so you want to save the original document as a version so you can quickly go back to it if the plans fall through.

What You Do	How You Do It
1. Identify Revise Management.doc as the original version of the document.	a. Open Revise Management.doc. b. Choose File→Versions. c. Click Save Now. d. In the Comments On Version text box, type *original management team*. e. Click OK.
2. Save a new version of the document without the Relocation Services management paragraph.	a. Delete the paragraph beginning "In Relocation Services...". b. Choose File→Versions. c. Click Save Now. d. In the Comments box, type *new management team*. e. Click OK.
3. Display the original version of the document.	a. Choose File→Versions. b. Select the original version. c. Click Open.

4. How many versions of the document are open?

___

5. Close both versions of the document.	a. Click the Close button in the top window.
	b. Click the Close button in the bottom window.
	c. Restore the document window.

TOPIC B

Distribute a Document

It's always important to be able to edit your own documents, but sometimes, it helps to have others edit your documents for you. Before they can make suggestions for improvement, they have to receive your document. In this topic, you'll distribute your document so that co-workers can review it.

These days, it's probable that members of a project team work in different offices or even in different time zones. While it might seem like a hassle gathering email addresses or putting your document on a server, it's a lot less hassle to distribute your documents electronically than it is to distribute them in person, especially if someone you're working with lives across the country.

The Collaboration Process

Here is an overview of the collaboration process.

Stage	Description
1. Protect the Document	You add security to your document. Before you distribute your document to others, you want to ensure that only the people who should have access to your document can open it and that any changes they make to that document are tracked.
2. Distribute the Document	You send your document to the other members of your team. To get your document to the other members of your team, you can: • Send the document as an email attachment. • Post the document on a shared network server.
3. Revise the Document	The members of your project team make changes to your document.
4. Review Changes	You review and accept or reject the changes suggested by the members of your project team.

Document Security Options

From the Security tab in the Options dialog box (see Figure 5-2), you can access several different ways you can protect your documents. You can:

- Require a password to open the document. You can use the Security tab in the Options dialog box to set a password that users must enter in order to open the document.

- Require a password to edit the document. You can also use the Security tab to set a password users must enter in order to make changes to the document.

- Recommend that users open the file as a read-only file.

- Add a digital signature to the document.

- Protect the document so that users cannot make changes to the document without tracking revisions.

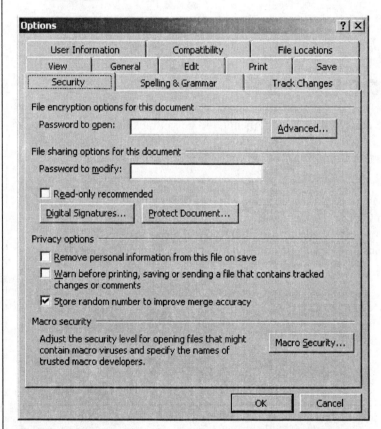

Figure 5-2: *The Security tab in the Options dialog box.*

Protect a Document from Editing

Procedure Reference: Protect a Document

You can protect a document by adding a password to it so that users cannot revise the document without tracking the changes they make to it. To protect a document:

1. Choose Tools→Protect Document.

2. Verify that the Tracked Changes option is selected in the Protect Document For section.

3. Enter a password for the document.

4. Click OK.

5. Re-enter the password and click OK.

When you send the document to other members of your team for review, Word will track every change they make to the document unless they know the password that enables them to turn off the Track Changes option.

Create Digital Signatures

With Microsoft Word XP, you can create a digital certificate to digitally sign a file. The certificate confirms that you created the document and that it has not been changed since you attached your signature to it.

To create a digital signature:

1. Run Selfcert.exe (you can double-click on it in the Windows Explorer).

2. Enter your name and click OK to create a digital signature for your name.

3. Click OK to close the SelfCert Success dialog box.

When you save a document that has a digital signature, Word removes the digital signature from the document.

Attach Digital Signatures

The digital signature you create with the selfcert.exe tool that ships with Office XP does not create a valid certificate; however, you can use it to ensure that the documents you create are not tampered with by anyone but you. To add a digital signature to a document:

1. In the document you want to add the digital signature to, choose Tools→Options and display the Security tab.

2. Click the Digital Signatures button to open the Digital Signature dialog box.

3. Click the Add button to open the Select Certificate dialog box.

4. Select the certificate you want to use for your digital signature and click OK.

5. Click OK to close the Digital Signature dialog box.

6. Click OK to close the Options dialog box. The text "(signed)" appears next to the document title in the Title bar and a certificate icon appears in the Status bar.

The digital certificate you create using the Selfcert.exe tool attaches a certificate icon with a red X mark next Digital Signature dialog box. The red X indicates that this certificate is unauthenticated. If you want an authentic certificate, you must either purchase one from a certification authority (such as VeriSign) or from your company's security administrator.

ACTIVITY 5-2

Securing Your Document

Data Files:

- Stockholder Review.doc

Scenario:

Before you distribute a document to others, you want to make sure that only the people who are authorized to do so can open the document. You decide to protect the document so that any changes made to the document are tracked. In addition, your workgroup has decided it's a good idea to add a digital signature to group documents so that everyone will know the document is authentic. You want to save the original unprotected document, so after you add security, you save the file as My Stockholder Review.

What You Do	How You Do It
1. Protect Stockholder Review.doc with the password *sharing*.	a. Open Stockholder Review.doc.
	b. Choose Tools→Options.
	c. Display the Security tab.
	d. In the Password To Open text box, **type** *sharing*.
	e. **Click OK.**
	f. In the Confirm Password dialog box, **type** *sharing* **and click OK.**
	g. Save the file as *My Stockholder Review*.
2. Test the password to make sure that it works.	a. Close My Stockholder Review.doc.
	b. Open My Stockholder Review.doc.
	c. Type the password *sharing* and click OK.

3. **Create a digital signature.**

   a. **Choose Start→Run and click Browse** to find the SelfCert.exe file. (You may find it in the C:\Program Files\Microsoft Office\ Office 10 folder.)

   b. **Double-click on SelfCert.exe** to place it in the Open text box in the Run dialog box.

   c. **Click OK.**

   d. **Type your name and click OK.**

   e. **Click OK** to close the SelfCert Success dialog box.

4. **Add a digital signature to the document and save the file.**

   a. **Choose Tools→Options** and, if necessary, **display the Security tab.**

   b. **Click the Digital Signatures button.**

   c. **Click the Add button** and, if necessary, **click Yes.**

   d. If necessary, **select your name and click OK.**

   e. **Click OK** to close the Digital Signature dialog box.

   f. **Click OK** to close the Options dialog box.

   g. **Save the file.**

5. **Protect the document so that any changes will be tracked and save the file.**

   a. **Choose Tools→Protect Document.**

   b. In the Password text box, **enter a password.**

   c. **Click OK.**

   d. **Enter the password again and click OK.**

   e. **Save and close the file.**

    Saving the file removes the digital signature.

Distribute a Document for Review

Procedure Reference: Send a Document by Email

To distribute your document to the other members of your team, you can place it on a network server to which they have access, or you can send the document to them by using email. To send the document by email:

1. Open the document you want to send.

2. Click the E-mail button.

3. In the To and Cc fields, enter the email address of the persons to whom you want to send the document.

4. In the Introduction text box, enter any comments or explanations.

5. Click the Send A Copy button.

OPTIONAL ACTIVITY 5-3

Distributing the Document for Review

Data Files:

- Sharing.doc

Setup:

You need a partner to whom you will send the document. You must also have Outlook set up and an Exchange server if you plan to complete this activity.

Scenario:

Now that you've protected your document, you're ready to distribute it to the people you want to review it. You know that you can send the document as an email, and you decide to do that.

What You Do	How You Do It
1. Send the document Sharing.doc to a member of your class.	a. Open Sharing.
	b. On the Standard toolbar, **click the E-mail button.**
	c. In the To text box, **enter your partner's name.**
	d. In the Introduction text box, **type** *This is the document I'd like you to review.*
	e. **Click the Send A Copy button.**
	f. **Close the document.**

TOPIC C

Track Changes to a Document

Now that you know how to distribute your document, you want to set the revision tracking so that you can take full advantage of the collaboration capabilities of Word. In this topic, you will set the revision tracking so that any changes made by others will be tracked.

You've shared your document. Others can now make changes to it. You are worried that when all those co-workers make their changes, you won't have any idea who made what changes. For example, you want to be sure to implement the changes that your boss suggested, but the changes that your peers suggest may not be valuable to you. If you set revision tracking, you will know who is making what changes and you will then be able to go through and decide which revisions to implement and which to reject.

Word's Track Changes Feature

Word's Track Changes command enables you to keep track of revisions to documents. When you activate this command, Word marks all changes made to a document in different colors, with one color assigned to each person who works on the document. In Print Layout view, text you insert is underlined, balloon captions show comments and text that has been deleted, formatted, and so on. A vertical line in the left margin shows where revisions have been made to the original document.

Track Document Changes

Procedure Reference: Track Changes to a Document

One way you can track the revisions that members of your team make to your document is to track changes as they are made.

1. Open the document you want to revise.

2. Enable the Track Changes feature:
   - Choose Tools→Track Changes.
   - Double-click on the TRK indicator on the Status bar.

   The TRK indicator on the Status bar indicates revision tracking is active.

ACTIVITY 5-4

Tracking Changes While Editing a Document

Data Files:

- Edit and Track Changes.doc

Scenario:

You've been asked to review a document created by a member of your team. Your team member didn't force the issue, but asked you to use Word's revision tracking feature for any changes you make to the document. As you review the document, you decide that the tag line isn't really necessary, so you delete it. When you're finished, save the document as My Edit and Tracking.

What You Do	How You Do It
1. In Edit and Track Changes.doc , turn on revision tracking.	a. Open Edit and Track Changes.doc.
	b. Choose Tools→Track Changes.
2. On screen, is there a way that you can tell revision tracking is enabled?	

3. Delete the tag line and save and close the file.

   a. Select the text "We find the right property for you."

   b. Press [Delete].

   c. Scroll down and view the comments. The comment text appears in a balloon on the right side of the document.

   d. Save the file as *My Edit and Tracking* and close the file.

TOPIC D

Review Document Changes

You know how to use Word's revision tracking feature to track changes to a document, but what do you do when you get a document that's full of changes? In this topic, you will review changes and decide whether or not to incorporate them in the document.

Whenever you ask someone to review something for you, they are bound to make suggestions that you don't like or that are not appropriate, as well as those that are wonderful. If you don't know how to accept or reject changes, you'll wind up with a document that is a mass of colors and doesn't make much sense.

The Reviewing Toolbar

Reviewing revision marks and accepting or rejecting changes that other members of your team propose can be overwhelming. You can use the tools on the Reviewing toolbar, shown in Figure 5-3, to examine and work with revisions.

Figure 5-3: *The tools on the Reviewing toolbar.*

Review Changes

Procedure Reference: Review Changes to a Document

To review changes to a document:

1. Open the document that contains the revision marks.

2. Turn on the Change Tracking feature, if necessary.

3. On the Reviewing toolbar, click the Previous or Next button to select a revision.

4. Click the Accept Change or Reject Change/Delete Comment button to accept or reject the change.

ACTIVITY 5-5

Accepting and Rejecting Changes to a Document

Data Files:

- Reviewed.doc

Scenario:

You received changes from each member of your team. Now you're ready to review and accept or reject the suggestions. When you're finished, save the file as My Reviewed.

What You Do	How You Do It
1. Scroll through the document and observe the changes. **What types of changes appear in balloons?** **Who deleted the sentence in the Our Goal section? How could you tell?**	
2. In the Reviewed.doc file, **accept the first and second changes.**	a. **Open Reviewed.doc.** b. On the Reviewing toolbar, **click the Next button.** c. **Click the Accept Change button.** d. **Click the Next button.** e. **Click the Accept Change button.**
3. **Reject the third change.**	a. **Click the Next button.** b. **Click the Reject Change/Delete Comment button.**

4. **Continue through the document accepting and rejecting changes.**

   a. **Click Next and click Accept Change or Reject Change** to accept or reject the changes.

   b. **Continue clicking Next and Accept Change or Reject Change** until you reach the end of the document.

   c. **Save the document as** *My Reviewed*.

   d. **Close the document.**

Lesson 5 Follow-up

Working with others is an important part of life today. The easier it is to collaborate with the people around you, the more likely you are to be productive in your job. In this lesson, you learned how to create document versions, distribute a document for editing, track changes to a document, and respond to suggested changes in your documents.

1. **Which of the techniques presented in this lesson are you most likely to use on your job?**

2. **How do you work with others on documents in your workplace?**

NOTES

LESSON 6
Modifying an HTML Page

Lesson Objectives:

In this lesson, you will modify an HTML page in Word.

You will:

- Save a Word document as an HTML file.
- Edit an HTML page in Word.
- Create scrolling text on a Web page.
- Insert a movie clip on a Web page.
- Insert a sound file in a Web page.

Introduction

You already know how to use Word to create a Web page. In this lesson, you'll use Word to modify existing Web pages.

Suppose you have a Web page and you just need to make a few minor tweaks. You could open the page in some text editor and try to wade through the HTML tags, or you could open the page in Word and edit in Word's What You See Is What You Get (WYSIWYG) interface.

TOPIC A

Save Word Documents as Web Pages

You know that you can use a wizard to create new Web pages using Word. In this topic, you will save an existing Word document as an HTML file.

You spend a long time creating and formatting a document so that it looks exactly the way you want it to, and you then find that you need to display that document on an intranet or the Internet. What do you do? Create the document all over in FrontPage? No. All you need to do is save the Word document as a Web page. Word does all the work for you.

Create a Web Page

Procedure Reference: Save a Word Document as an HTML Page

To save a Word document as an HTML page:

1. Create and format the document as desired.

2. Choose File→Save As Web Page.

3. In the File Name text box, name the file.

4. Click the Change Title button to open the Set Page Title dialog box.

5. Enter a title you want displayed in the Title bar when you open the Web page in a browser.

6. Click OK. Word displays the title you set above the File Name text box.

7. Click Save.

DISCOVERY ACTIVITY 6-1

Saving a Word Document as a Web Page

Scenario:

You have a document that you've spent a long time creating and formatting in Word. You plan to send it out to customers, but your manager also thinks it would be a great idea to display the document on the company Web site. You agree that it would be and decide to make it happen by saving the Word document as a Web page.

1. **Save Burke Home as a Web page and preview it in your browser.**

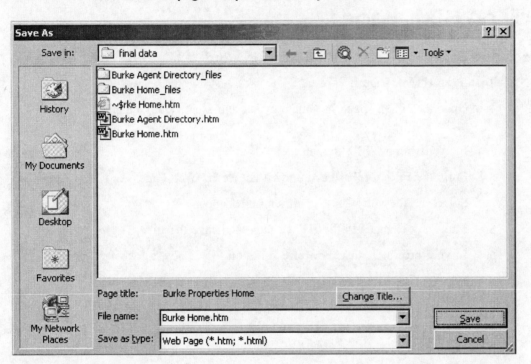

TOPIC B

Edit Web Pages in Word

You know that you can use Word to create Web pages, but did you know that you can also edit HTML pages in Word? In this topic you will make changes to the HTML document in Word.

If you just want to make a simple edit to a Web page, it's a real hassle to wade through all the tags to try to find what you want to change. And, if you mess up one tag, you might spend hours trying to figure out what you missed. Fortunately, with Office XP, you can use Word's intuitive user interface to make changes to your HTML documents.

Edit an HTML Page

Procedure Reference: Edit an HTML Page in Word

To edit an HTML page in Word:

1. Open the HTML page in your browser and identify any changes you want to make.

2. In Word, choose File→Open.

3. From the Files Of Type drop-down list, select Web Pages And Web Archives.

4. Select the file you want to edit, and click Open.

5. Make any changes to the HTML page and save the file.

6. In your browser, click the Refresh button to see how the changes look.

7. Repeat steps 5 and 6 until you're happy with your HTML page.

ACTIVITY 6-2

Editing an HTML Document in Word

Data Files:

- Burke Agent Directory.htm

Scenario:

You have an HTML document containing the names and addresses of all the Burke Properties agents. One of the Orlando agents left the company, so you need to remove him from the phone list. When you're finished, view the document in a browser to make sure that the change looks okay.

What You Do	How You Do It
1. In your browser, **open Burke Agent Directory.htm.**	a. **Start Internet Explorer.**
	b. **Choose File→Open.**
	c. **Click Browse.**
	d. From the My Documents folder, **select Burke Agent Directory.htm and click Open.**
	e. **Click OK.**
	f. **Scroll to find the Orlando agents.** Ian Yaworski left the company.
2. In Word, **delete Ian Yaworski from the Agents directory.**	a. **Switch to Word.**
	b. **Open Burke Properties Agents.htm.**
	c. **Delete Ian Yaworksi's information.**
	d. **Save the file.**

3. **View the changes in your browser.**

   a. **Switch to your browser.**

   b. **Click the Refresh button.**

   c. **Scroll to find the Orlando reps.** Ian Yaworski is no longer listed.

   d. **Close your browser.**

   e. **Close the file.**

TOPIC C

Insert Scrolling Text

As browsers become more sophisticated and computers become more powerful, multimedia elements—such as scrolling text, movies, and sound—they are becoming more common in Web pages. In the next few topics, you will learn how to use Word to add these multimedia elements to your Web pages. In this topic, you will add scrolling text to a Web page.

If you're looking to display breaking or frequently updated news on your Web page, scrolling text is the perfect choice to draw attention to that news.

Scrolling Text

Procedure Reference: Insert Scrolling Text

To insert scrolling text in a Web page:

1. Place the insertion point where you want to enter the scrolling text.
2. Display the Web Tools toolbar.
3. Click the Scrolling Text button.
4. In the Scrolling Text dialog box, from the Behavior drop-down list, select Slide to have the text slide onto the screen and stop.
5. From the Background Color drop-down list, select a background color for the scrolling text.
6. In the Type The Scrolling Text Here text box, type the text you want to scroll onto the screen.
7. Click OK to insert the scrolling text element.
8. Choose File→Web Page Preview to preview the Web page in a browser.
9. Close the browser and return to Word.

Format Scrolling Text

Scrolling text takes the format of the paragraph at the location of the insertion point. So, it's a good idea to format the paragraph before you insert the scrolling text. However, if you decide you want to change the format of the scrolling text after you have inserted it, you can do so in Design mode. To change the format of scrolling text,

1. On the Web Tools toolbar, click the Design button.

2. Select the scrolling text object you want to format.

3. Use the Font dialog box or the Formatting toolbar to format the text as desired.

4. Click the Design button to return to Run mode.

ACTIVITY 6-3

Inserting Scrolling Text in a Web Page

Data Files:

- Burke Properties Home.htm

Scenario:

You've been asked to update the Burke Properties Home Page. Because this is the 50th anniversary of the company, you decide to jazz up the Web page a little by adding scrolling text that lets visitors to the Web page know that fact.

LESSON 6

What You Do	How You Do It
1. In Burke Properties Home.htm , insert scrolling text as shown here.	a. **Open Burke Properties Home.htm** and **place the insertion point on the line between the heading and the navigation table.**

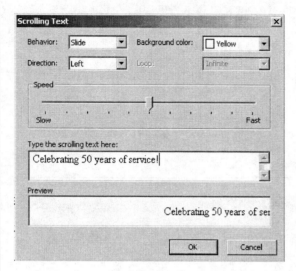

	b. **Display the Web Tools toolbar.**
	c. **Click the Scrolling Text button** [icon] .
	d. From the Behavior drop-down list, **select Slide** to make the text slide onto the screen and stop.
	e. From the Background Color drop-down list, **select Yellow.**
	f. In the Type The Scrolling Text Here text box, **select the text and type** *Celebrating 50 years of service!*
	g. **Click OK** to insert the scrolling text element.
	h. **Choose File→Web Page Preview** to preview the Web page in a browser. When you're finished, **close the browser and return to Word.**
	i. **Save the file as** *My Burke Properties Home.htm*.
2. **Change the formatting of the scrolling text to 48 point Times New Roman.**	a. **Click the Design Mode button** [icon]
	b. **Change the font size to 48 point.**
	c. **Click the Design Mode button** **again.**

3. Does it appear on-screen as though you have increased the point size that much?

4. **Use the Reveal Formatting task pane to check the point size for the scrolling text.**

   a. With the document still in Design mode, choose Format→Reveal Formatting to display the Formatting task pane.

   b. Under Font, verify that the point size is set to 48 pt.

   c. Close the Reveal Formatting task pane.

5. **View the scrolling text in your browser and then close the document without saving.**

   a. Choose File→Web Page Preview. The scrolling text does appear at its actual size in the browser window.

   b. Close the browser.

   c. Close the document without saving changes.

TOPIC D

Place a Movie Clip in a Web Page

Movies are another way you can add interest to your Web pages and documents. In this topic, we'll insert a movie clip in a Web page.

If you've gone to the trouble of creating a Web page, you want people to visit that page. A well-done movie can grab visitors to your Web site and pull them in. It can also efficiently explain something that might otherwise require a lot of text.

Insert Movie Clips

Procedure Reference: Insert a Movie Clip

To insert a movie clip in a Web page:

1. Place the insertion point where you want the movie to appear.

2. If necessary, display the Web Tools toolbar.

3. Click the Movie button.

4. In the Movie Clip dialog box, select the movie you want.

5. Set any options.

6. Click OK and preview the movie in a browser.

In the Movie Clip dialog box, you can select an alternate image and text if desired. These will be displayed if a visitor's browser is, for some reason, unable to play movie clips.

ACTIVITY 6-4

Placing a Movie Clip in the Burke Properties Home Page

Data Files:

* Burke Movie.avi

Scenario:

Your manager created a little custom movie that introduces Burke Properties' moving services. You want to include the movie clip at the beginning of the Relocation Help section of the Web page.

What You Do	How You Do It
1. In My Burke Properties.htm, before the Relocation Help heading, **insert a movie clip that runs when you click the mouse.**	a. **Open My Burke Properties.htm.**
	b. **Scroll down to find the Relocation Help heading.**
	c. **Click the Movie button** 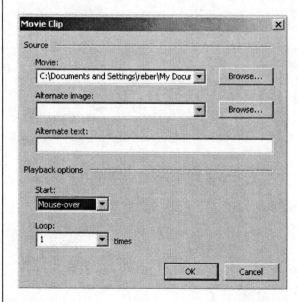 .
	d. **In the Movie Clip dialog box, next to the Movie drop-down list, click the Browse button.**
	e. **Double-click on Burke Movie.avi.**
	f. **From the Start drop-down list, select Mouse-Over** to run the movie one time when a user moves the mouse pointer over it.
	g. **Click OK and click Continue** to insert the movie clip.
	h. **Preview the page in a browser and run the movie clip.**
	i. **Close the browser and return to Word.**

TOPIC E

Insert a Background Sound

You may have visited a Web site that made noises or played music as you browsed through it. Sound is another way to add interest to your Web pages. In this topic, you'll learn how to add a sound to your Web page.

Used appropriately, sound can enhance a user's perception of your Web site. It can add a professional touch to your Web site.

Add Sound to a Web Page

Procedure Reference: Insert a Sound

To insert a sound in a Web page:

1. Place the insertion point where you want to insert the sound.

2. On the Web Tools toolbar, click the Sound button.

3. In the Background Sound dialog box, next to the Sound drop-down list, click the Browse button.

4. Double-click on the sound you want to insert.

5. In the Loop text box, set the number of times you want the sound to play.

6. Click OK.

7. Preview the Web page in a browser to test the sound.

8. Close the browser and return to Word.

OPTIONAL ACTIVITY 6-5

Inserting Sound into a Web Page

Data Files:

- Burke Sound.wav

Setup:

If you choose to complete this optional activity, you will hear the sound only if your computer has a sound card installed. My Burke Properties.htm is open.

Scenario:

Recently you've been out surfing the Web and you noticed that most sites have sound. You decide to add a sound clip to the Burke Properties Home Page that will greet visitors when they open the page.

What You Do	How You Do It
1. At the beginning of the Burke Properties Home Page, **insert the Burke Sound.wav file.**	a. **Place the insertion point at the beginning of the document.**
	b. **Click the Sound button** .
	c. **In the Background Sound dialog box, click the Browse button next to the Sound drop-down list.**
	d. **Double-click on the Burke Sound.wav file.**
	e. **Click OK to insert the sound.**
	f. **Preview the Web page in a browser.**
	g. **Close the browser and return to Word.**
	h. **Save and close the file and exit Word.**

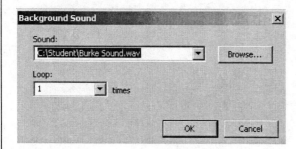

Lesson 6 Follow-up

Congratulations! You now know about some of the ways you can use Word to edit and modify your HTML pages. You can view your Web page in any browser and re-open it and make any modifications you want in Word, and then re-open the page in your browser without losing any formatting.

1. **What types of Web pages might you modify in Word?**

2. **What are some ways you can use Word to customize your Web pages?**

Follow-up

Congratulations. You're now ready to go out and continue to learn about Microsoft Word. In this course, you learned how to create and distribute custom forms, how to write and revise macros, how to create references to information within your documents, as well as how to create a table of contents and index for your documents. You also learned how to use Word's collaboration tools to work with those around you to create and edit documents. Finally, you learned how to make changes to your HTML pages in Word.

1. **How is this course most likely to change the way you use Microsoft Word.**

2. **What projects are you going to use Microsoft Word to complete in the next month?**

What's Next?

This is the last course in the series for Microsoft Word for Windows. When you finish this course, you can check the Element K Web site for additional courses on specific Word for Windows topics.

APPENDIX A
Microsoft Office Specialist Program

Selected Element K courseware addresses Microsoft Office Specialist skills. The following tables indicate where Word 2002 skills are covered. For example, 1-3 indicates the lesson and activity number applicable to that skill.

Core Skill Sets and Skills Being Measured	Word 2002: Level 1	Word 2002: Level 2	Word 2002: Level 3
Inserting and Modifying Text			
Insert, modify, and move text and symbols	1-2, 1-6, 2-6, 3-7, 6-5		
Apply and modify text formats	3-1		
Correct spelling and grammar usage	6-6, 6-7		
Apply font and text effects	3-1, 3-2, 3-4		
Enter and format Date and Time	6-4		
Apply character styles		1-2	
Creating and Modifying Paragraphs			
Modify paragraph formats	4-1, 4-2, 4-3, 4-6, 4-7		
Set and modify tabs	4-5, 4-5		
Apply bullet, outline, and numbering format to paragraphs	4-8, 4-9, 4-10		
Apply paragraph styles		1-1	
Formatting Documents			
Create and modify a header and footer	7-3		
Apply and modify column settings	7-6	4-2, 4-3	
Modify document layout and Page Setup options	7-2, 7-3, 7-4, 7-5		

APPENDIX A

Core Skill Sets and Skills Being Measured	Word 2002: Level 1	Word 2002: Level 2	Word 2002: Level 3
Create and modify tables	5-1, 5-2, 5-3, 5-4, 5-5, 5-6		
Preview and Print documents, envelopes, and labels	7-1, 7-7	4-5	
Managing Documents			
Manage files and folders for documents	1-3		
Create documents using templates	6-1		
Save documents using different names and file formats	1-3		
Working with Graphics			
Insert images and graphics		3-1	
Create and modify diagrams and charts		3-4	
Workgroup Collaboration			
Compare and Merge documents		7-2, 7-3	
Insert, view, and edit comments		7-1	
Convert documents into Web pages		6-1, 6-2	

Expert Skill Sets And Skills Being Measured	Word 2002: Level 1	Word 2002: Level 2	Word 2002: Level 3
Customizing Paragraphs			
Control Pagination	7-5	4-3	
Sort paragraphs in lists and tables		2-4	
Formatting documents			
Create and format document sections		1-1, 4-1	
Create and apply character and paragraph styles		1-1, 1-2, 1-4	
Create and update document indexes and tables of contents, figures, and authorities			4-3, 4-6, 4-7
Create cross-references			3-5
Add and revise endnotes and footnotes			3-2, 3-3
Create and manage master documents and subdocuments			4-8
Move within documents			3-1
Create and modify forms using various form controls			1-1, 1-2, 1-3, 1-4

Expert Skill Sets And Skills Being Measured	Word 2002: Level 1	Word 2002: Level 2	Word 2002: Level 3
Create forms and prepare forms for distribution			1-6, 1-7
Customizing Tables			
Use Excel data in tables		2-7	
Perform calculations in Word tables		2-2, 2-5	
Creating and Modifying Graphics			
Create, modify, and position graphics		3-1, 3-2, 3-3	
Create and modify charts using data from other applications		2-6	
Align text and graphics		4-4	
Customizing Word			
Create, edit, and run macros			2-1, 2-2, 2-3
Customize menus and toolbars			2-5, 2-6, 2-7
Workgroup Collaboration			
Track, accept, and reject changes to documents			5-4, 5-5
Merge input from several reviewers		7-2, 7-3	5-3
Insert and modify hyperlinks to other documents and web pages		6-3, 6-4	
Create and edit Web documents in Word			6-1, 6-2
Create document versions			5-1
Protect documents			5-2
Define and modify default file locations for workgroup templates			6-2
Attach digital signatures to documents			5-2
Using Mail Merge			
Merge letters with a Word, Excel, or Access data source		5-2, 5-3, 5-4, 5-6, 5-7, 5-8	
Merge labels with a Word, Excel, or Access data source		5-9	
Use Outlook data as mail merge data source		5-2, 5-3, 5-4, 5-5, 5-6, 5-7, 5-8	

NOTES

LESSON LABS

Due to classroom setup constraints, some labs cannot be keyed in sequence immediately following their associated lesson. Your instructor will tell you whether your labs can be practiced immediately following the lesson or whether they require separate setup from the main lesson content.

LESSON 1 LAB 1

Creating and Distributing Forms

Scenario:

Your manager at Books & Beyond has decided to let customers evaluate books & CD's before they purchase them. Rather than continue using the current sign up sheet, she wants you to design a form that will include more information about the lender and materials that were signed out. Using your experience in creating forms, create a form template that looks like the following graphic.

Books·&·Beyond¶

Book·&·CD·Loan·Form¶
¶

Customer·Information¶

Name⌷	⌷	⌷
Address⌷	⌷	⌷
Phone·Number⌷	⌷	⌷
Book/CD·Title⌷	⌷	⌷
Sign·Out·Date⌷	⌷	⌷
Sign·In·Date⌷	⌷	⌷
Materials·Returned:⌷	⌷	⌷
Materials·Purchased:⌷	⌷	⌷

¶

1. Using the graphic above as a reference, create the table and enter the text in each cell.

2. Save the form as the *My Signout* template.

3. Insert the form fields of your choice into the template.

4. Test the form and then close it without saving.

LESSON 2 LAB 1

Automating Tasks

Scenario:

Your manager's correspondence consists mostly of memos, so she has asked you to help speed up the process by automating the procedure. Since you've had some experience creating macros, naturally she's come to you for help. Your going to record a macro that assigns the standard memorandum information to a menu. You'll create a macro that stores the memo information shown in the graphic below.

```
Interoffice·Memorandum¶
¶
¶
¶
To: →      →    ]¶
From:→   →    ¶
Date:→    →    ¶
Subject:   →    ¶
¶
¶
¶
```

1. In a new blank document, in the Record Macro dialog box, name the macro and give it a description.

2. Enter the information shown in the graphic above.

3. Test the macro.

4. Edit the macro so that the heading is centered and the current date is automatically inserted.

5. Add the macro to a new menu of your choice and then test the macro.

6. Close any open documents.

LESSON 3 LAB 1

Referencing Document Information

Scenario:

Your manager has a new assignment for you. She has a 2-page document that she constantly refers to and needs you to make finding information easier. You're going to add a bookmark, figure caption, and cross-reference to the document.

1. In *Reference Practice*, bookmark "Other Special Services."

2. Use the bookmark to move quickly to the "Other Special Services" heading .

3. Create a caption for the diagram located on page 1.

4. Create a cross-reference to the table located on page 2.

5. Save the file as *My Reference Practice* and then close it.

LESSON 4 LAB 1

Preparing a Document for Publication

Scenario:

Your manager has a 4 page document that needs some finishing touches before it is handed out at the meeting later in the day. For your next assignment, you'll add odd and even page headers, a table of contents, and an index to the document.

1. In *Publication Practice*, create odd and even page headers and footers of your choice.

2. Create a table of contents for the document that looks like the following graphic.

3. Create an index for the document that looks like the following graphic.

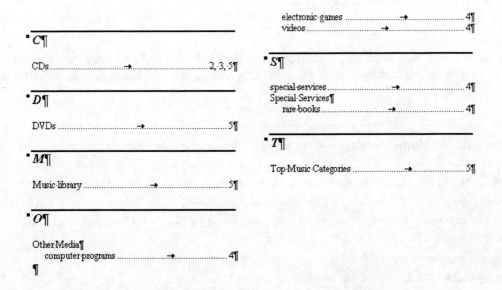

4. Save the file as *My Publication Practice* and then close it.

LESSON 5 LAB 1

Revising Documents

Scenario:

Your manager has just finished reviewing your document and she has made some suggested changes and additions to it. Using Word's reviewing toolbar, accept and or reject any changes you find necessary to the document.

1. In Reviewing Practice, turn on the Change Tracking feature.

2. Use the buttons on the Reviewing toolbar to review the changes and accept or reject changes as you see fit.

3. Continue reviewing until you reach the end of the document.

4. Save the document as *My Reviewing Practice* and then close it.

LESSON 6 LAB 1

Modifying an HTML page

Scenario:

You've put a lot of work into the document about Books & Beyond and your manager thinks it should be put on the company Web site. You're going to save the document as a Web page and add some scrolling text to it.

1. **Open Books Home and save it as a Web page called *My Books Home*.**

2. **Edit the HTML document in Word by removing the pyramid diagram.**

3. **Insert scrolling text as shown in the graphic and change the font and size to one of your choice.**

4. **View the Web page in your browser and then save and close the document.**

SOLUTIONS

Lesson 1

Activity 1-2

3. **How can you display the field code?**

    Press [Alt][F9] to toggle between the field code and the default prompt.

Activity 1-6

1. **What are some reasons you might want to protect a form?**

    You can't edit information in the fields until you protect the form, and if you don't protect the form, anyone who uses it can modify your form in any way.

3. **How can you tell whether the form is protected or not?**

    You can't click anywhere except in the fields, and when you click in the Drop-Down form field for Property Type, a down arrow appears to the right of the first entry "Single Family."

5. **Now that you've entered a password for the form, what happens when you click the Protect Form button?**

    Word displays a dialog box asking for the password. When you enter the correct password and click OK, Word unprotects the form.

Activity 1-7

2. **Is there any information you couldn't enter?**

    Yes. It was difficult to indicate that Lydia has no preference for the type of property she would like to purchase.

Lesson 2

Activity 2-1

2. **How is the company referred to in the document?**

   The company is referred to as both "Burke Properties, Inc." and "Burke Properties." Neither reference to the company includes the trademark symbol.

4. **Now how is the company referred to throughout the document?**

   Each reference to the company appears as Burke Properties and is followed by the trademark symbol.

Activity 2-3

2. **Using Figure 2-2 as a guide, identify the components of the Visual Basic Editor.**

   a Code window   *b* Project Explorer

   c Project   *d* Modules

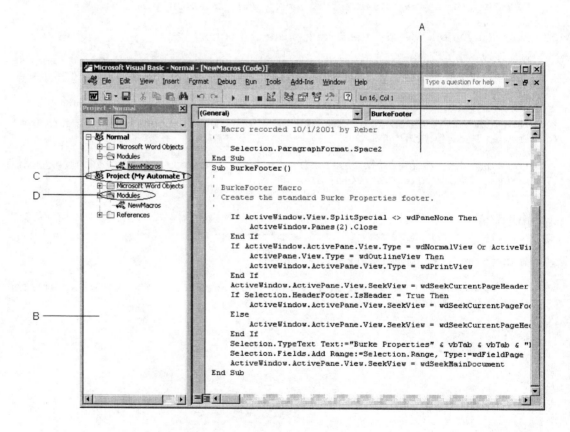

Lesson 3

Activity 3-1

3. **How many bookmarks are in the document?**

There are three bookmarks in the document.

Can you tell by looking at the document that it contains bookmarks?

Currently, you cannot tell by looking at the document, but you might have noticed that there were three bookmarks listed in the Enter Bookmark Name drop-down list.

Activity 3-2

4. **What page of the document does the endnote appear on?**

The endnote appears at the top of page 8.

Activity 3-4

3. **How did the figure number for the organization chart change?**

When you added a caption to the first figure, Word renumbered the organization chart as Figure 2.

Lesson 4

Activity 4-4

3. **How has the table of contents changed?**

The new heading, Management Team, appears before the Outlook heading in the table of contents, and the page number for the Outlook section has changed.

Activity 4-6

4. **How can you tell Word has marked the index entries in the document?**

A field {XE"index entry word" } appears in the text wherever Word has marked an index entry.

Will these index entries print in the document? Why or why not?

The index entries are hidden text. They will not print unless you specify in the Print dialog box that hidden text should print.

Activity 4-7

2. How does the relocation services entry you created in the concordance file appear in the index?

"Relocation" is indented below "services."

Activity 4-8

3. How does this document look different from the documents you usually work on?

There is a section break above and below it, and a border around the subdocument text.

Lesson 5

Activity 5-1

4. How many versions of the document are open?

Both versions are open.

Activity 5-4

2. On screen, is there a way that you can tell revision tracking is enabled?

The TRK indicator in the Status bar indicates that the Track Changes feature is on.

Activity 5-5

1. What types of changes appear in balloons?

Deletions and formatting changes appear in balloons on the right side of the screen.

Who deleted the sentence in the Our Goal section? How could you tell?

Lydia. When you move the mouse pointer over the change, Word displays the name of the reviewer and the date and time the change was made.

Lesson 6

Activity 6-3

3. **Does it appear on-screen as though you have increased the point size that much?**

   No. While the point size did increase, it doesn't look like it increased as much as it should have.

NOTES

GLOSSARY

bookmark
A placeholder used to mark a location in a document so that you can quickly return to that location.

concordance file
A Word document that consists of a two-column table. The first column of the table contains the words you want Word to search for and mark in your document. The second column contains the words as you want them to appear in the index.

cross-reference
A pointer in a document that refers to specific information in the same document or in another document. In Word, you can create cross-references for numbered items, headings, bookmarks, footnotes and endnotes, equations, figures, and tables.

endnote
A note, at the end of a section or of a document, that comments on or cites a reference for a particular fact in the text.

field codes
The code that tells Word what to do or display in a field.

fields
Containers for variable information in a document.

footnote
A note that appears at the bottom of a page and comments on or cites the reference for a particular fact in the text of a document.

form
A document that contains fields in which you enter information. A form consists of static text and fields.

gutter margin
Space added to the inside margin of a page so that the text isn't obscured by the binding method.

index
An alphabetical guide to words, phrases, and concepts in your documents. The index appears at the end of the document and indicates the page on which each word, phrase, or concept is located, so you can quickly find that information.

macro
A stored series of instructions that you can run by invoking a single command. You can use macros to standardize complex and repetitive tasks.

master document
A container that contains text and links to a series of related documents called subdocuments.

mirror margins
A feature that, when active, allows you to set the inside and outside margins for the right page while simultaneously creating a mirror image of those margin settings on the left page.

subdocuments
Documents linked to a master document.

table of contents
A list of the contents of a document generated by Word based on the built-in heading styles.

NOTES

INDEX

INDEX

footnotes
  defining, 50
  inserting, 51
Form Field buttons, 12
form fields, 7, 12
forms
  adding fields, 8, 9, 12
  creating a template, 3
  defining, 2
  locking, 18
  revising, 21
  setting field options, 13
  testing, 20
Forms toolbar, 12, 18

G
Go To dialog box, 47
gutter margins
  defining, 65
  setting, 65

H
Header And Footer toolbar, 67
headers, 67
HTML pages, 106

I
indexes
  defining, 75
  generating, 78
  marking, 76

M
macros
  assigning to a toolbar, 37
  creating a custom menu, 42
  defining, 26
  editing, 33, 34
  planning, 29
  recording, 29
  running, 26
  testing, 34
master documents, 83
  considering advantages, 82
  considering disadvantages, 82
  creating, 83
  creating from an existing document, 83
  creating from scratch, 83
  defining, 81
menus

  creating, 42
  deleting, 42
mirror margins
  defining, 64
  setting, 65
movie clips, 111, 112

O
odd headers and footers, 67
Options dialog box, 92

P
Protect Form button, 18

R
Reject Change/Delete Comment button, 99
Reviewing toolbar, 99

S
Save Now button, 89
scrolling text, 108
Security tab, 92
sound files, 113
subdocuments, 83
  defining, 81
  removing, 83

T
table of contents
  creating, 69
  modifying, 71, 73
  updating, 71
templates
  adding fields, 8, 9, 12
  creating, 3
  locking, 18
  revising, 21
  setting field options, 13
  testing, 20
Text form fields, 7
Track Changes option, 93, 97, 98
TRK indicator, 98

V
Versions dialog box, 89
Visual Basic Editor, 33

W
Web pages
  adding a movie clip, 111, 112

NOTES